JUN 0 3 2005

AGATHA CHRISTIE

A READER'S COMPANION

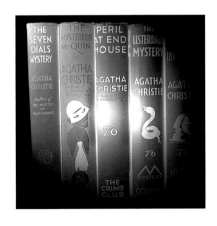

AGATHA CHRISTIE
A READER'S COMPANION

VANESSA WAGSTAFF & STEPHEN POOLE

AURUM PRESS

First published in Great Britain
2004 by Aurum Press Ltd
25 Bedford Avenue, London WC1B 3AT

ISBN 1 84513 015 4

1 3 5 7 9 8 6 4 2
2004 2006 2008 2007 2005

Printed in Singapore

Previous pages: Sunset on the west side of Burgh Island, Bigbury-On-Sea, South Devon.

CONTENTS

ACKNOWLEDGEMENTS

This book could not have been produced as it is without exceptional and generous assistance from the following persons:

Teresa Chris, literary agent, without whom this book would never have been published; Piers Burnett, editorial director at Aurum Press, for his never-ending patience, advice and eye for committing to our idea;

Matthew Prichard and Charity Massey at Chorion plc and Agatha Christie Ltd for giving their essential support; David Brawn at HarperCollins for all permissions granted; Denise Bontoft of Random House; John Mallowan for his generous permission to use family photographs of his uncle Max Mallowan and aunt Agatha Mallowan; Robert Updegraff and Louise Ang, for their valuable advice on technical aspects of book design; Henrietta McCall and Herma Chang at the British Museum for their generous time and advice with the Mallowan Album Collection; Bryony Kelly, formerly of the Royal Pharmaceutical Society, for her helpfulness concerning the museum's photographs and collection of poisons; David Suchet, Hugh Fraser and Sorcha Cusack for permission to use their photographs; Roxanne Harvey and Maxine Tate of Carnival Films, London; Charlotte Holdich for her donation of costume designs and longstanding helpfulness and advice; Carlotta Barrow, set designer, for her generous donation of photographs; Elizabeth Owen at Cosprop Ltd, London for her knowledge on period clothes and helpful contacts; Simon Bruntwood at Abney Hall, owned by Bruntwood Estates;

Alison Pickering and Ian Francis of OAG Company (formerly *The ABC Railway Guide)* for their time spent helping me photograph and reproduce details of the vintage editions; Frank Anderson and Peter Skinner at the Croydon Airport Society Archives for their very generous time, supplying the photographs and ephemeral material which make *Death in the Clouds* so lovely; Rex, son of Charles Morgan, for permission to use his father's photograph of Agatha Christie; David Reid and staff at Stockport Heritage Library, Stockport, for their generous use of archival photographs of Abney Hall; Jean Meillasoux and staff at the Orient Express Wagon Lits Companie, Paris, France; Karum Ram, archivist of Jaguar.com; Tony and Deborah Orchard of the Burgh Island Hotel for complete access to their property;

Staff at the Cambridge University Library for supplying most of the scans of rare book jackets; Mark Terry of Facsimile Book Jackets, California, for supplying original and near-impossible-to-find UK and US jacket scans from his archival collection; Brian Behrman for supplying some US book jackets and some vital scans of his UK collection and for his assistance with research; James Pickard (Rare Books) for supplying some unique fine jackets and bindings in his collection; Jon Gilbert and Jonathan Kearns of Adrian Harrington Rare Books; and Pablo Pico at Peter Harrington Rare Books for their forbearance in answering questions and time given to photography; Chris Fruin of LMS Books for all his generous help;

Staff at the Dartmouth Steam Railway; staff at the Salcombe Hotel, Salcombe, Devon, for supplying a history of the building and permission to photograph from the private hotel grounds; Daniel O'Brien at the Shapero Gallery for antique maps of Egypt; Roxanne Nash and Emma Baudey at Sotheran's Rare Books for time photographing their David Robert Prints collection; Sandra Bartlett, wig-room manageress at Ede & Ravenscroft, for advice on legal wigs; Rev. and Mrs Thomas Holmes of The Vicarage, Penshurst, Kent; Mr and Mrs J. M. C. Hall of Churston, Devon, for access to their modernist house and information on local architecture; Jane McMorland-Hunter, author of *Teach Yourself Series: Gardening, Needlecraft* and *Mosaics,* and her assistance with photography; Robert Innes-Smith; Gavin Pain of The Old Telephone Company, Battlebridge, Essex.

FOREWORD

Ever since I was a teenager there has been an Agatha Christie book in the house. Like many another reader I grew up with the Fontana paperbacks with their evocative Tom Adams artwork and fell in love easily with the vanished world brought to life in the stories.

In comparison with today, everything associated with that world seemed more beautiful and stylish. Even trains such as the Great Western's Cornish Riviera or the Southern's Brighton Belle seemed possessed of a drama and style alien to modern methods of transport. The books too, from the Golden Age of Detective Fiction, have an art-deco style conspicuously absent from so many twenty-first-century offerings; a style lovingly recreated in the feature films and television adaptations of both the Poirot and Miss Marple books, and to a lesser extent of the Tommy and Tuppence stories, which have done so much to introduce a new generation of readers to Agatha Christie.

After graduating from the Slade School of Fine Art, design became my focus and I set out determined, somehow, to enter the world of *Poirot*. After working as costume researcher on *Agatha Christie's Poirot*, amongst other TV period dramas, I decided to create a book, having satisfied myself that nothing similar existed, to do justice to the spirit of that vanished world. My friend and former colleague, Stephen Poole, was enthusiastic about the project and we decided to make it a joint venture. He would write the text and I would do everything else.

Lastly, I would like to dedicate this book to my mother and late father, without whose support and belief this book would never have been completed.   *VW*

Like Vanessa, I have always loved the works of the great detective writers from the Golden Age of Detective Fiction although, unlike Vanessa, I have afforded other writers such as Dorothy L. Sayers, Margery Allingham and Ngaio Marsh a status which she will only allow Agatha Christie. Contributing to this project has been a labour of love which has seemed barely a labour at all, so easily has it slotted into managing a central London multi-dealer antiquarian and rare book centre which has been from its foundation five years ago remarkably strong in Modern Firsts including classic Detective Fiction.

I must apologize to our readers for the unequal coverage of the books. Understandable constraints on space are to blame. Vanessa and I decided early on that we would feature most prominently the earlier books which many readers are unlikely to have seen in first edition let alone own, so prohibitive have prices become. Constraints on space have also led to some juggling with the order of the books, although only within their year of publication. I hope this concession will not prove too annoying. It remains only for me to thank Vanessa for her boundless enthusiasm and inspiration; my wife and children, particularly my daughter Kate, for their patient support and practical help; and our publishers for their constant encouragement.   *SP*

Vanessa Wagstaff and Stephen Poole, March 2004

INTRODUCTION
THE EARLY YEARS, 1890–1920

Opposite above: A local dispensary of the 1900s where all manner of drugs could be purchased, with lethal consequences if misused.

Opposite below: Although Agatha's heart was set in South Devon where she grew up, she had a life-long passion for Abney Hall, her brother-in-law's family seat, in Cheshire. The house constantly reappeared in numerous disguises in her novels. This is the lake, set in the grounds, which became the scene of the denouement in *They Do It With Mirrors.*

Agatha Christie died in 1976. She left behind a most impressive literary legacy of sixty-six crime novels and thirteen plays, as well as 154 short stories, most of which have been published in sixteen collections in the UK and thirteen in the USA. (A few stories have evaded publication as part of collections and are only available in their original serial form.) She also contributed to three collaborative detective novels and under the name of Mary Westmacott wrote six romantic novels.

A little over a quarter of a century after Christie's death, all her works published in book form remain in print in the UK and her most famous play, *The Mousetrap*, continues to delight audiences after more than 20,000 West End and countless amateur performances. Her works have been translated into more than fifty languages and published in seventy countries. She has sold over two billion books and her UK publisher, HarperCollins, expects to sell 600,000 each year. At least thirty feature films and over one hundred TV productions have been made and more are planned.

After such a recitation, it seems little less than amazing that her first book, *The Mysterious Affair at Styles*, should have been rejected by two major publishing houses, that nearly six years were to pass before it was eventually accepted by John Lane of The Bodley Head and that such a tight deal was struck that Christie made virtually no money and found herself contracted to offer her next five novels on terms only marginally better than those agreed for her first book.

Agatha Miller was born on 15 September 1890, the third and youngest child of an American, Frederick Miller, and his English wife Clarissa, at their recently acquired family home – Ashfield, a large comfortable villa in two acres of grounds in the genteel resort of Torquay on the south coast of Devon. Eight years younger than her next sibling Louis, Agatha saw little of her older brother and sister Madge, who were away at school much of the time, and was obliged to spend much time on her own or with a kind but elderly nanny. In consequence she found she had both to educate and to entertain herself. Her formal education did not begin until she was sixteen when she was sent to a

Above: Potassium cyanide, one of the most famous poisons in the history of detective fiction.

Right: Agatha at Paignton Zoo, Devon, with llamas, taken by Charles Morgan in the 1950s.

finishing school in Paris, for two years, followed by three months in Egypt with her widowed mother.

With her mother's encouragement, Agatha had already begun to write both stories and poetry. She had some success with her poems, some of which were published in *Poetry Review,* but fared less well with her short stories, which she regularly submitted without success to various magazines. She began a novel, which she entitled *Snow upon the Desert,* and solicited the help of a local author and family friend, Eden Phillpotts. He gave her advice and in due course the novel was submitted to his literary agent in London. But the interview between the literary agent and the budding young author was not a success and the novel was discarded.

Now in her early twenties, Agatha was in considerable demand by any number of young men and in due course, while engaged to someone else, she met and fell in love with a young officer in the Field Artillery, one Archie Christie. On Christmas Eve 1914, she married Christie, now a captain in the Royal Flying Corps. While her husband went off to fight the Germans, Agatha went to work at the Torbay Hospital in Torquay where she nursed the casualties returning from the Western Front. After two years of nursing, she graduated to the dispensary, where she acquired a knowledge of poisons that was to yield dividends in due course. She had already considered writing a detective novel, but her sister Madge was dismissive of the idea. Now, perhaps encouraged by the proximity of the poison cabinet, she decided to prove her sister wrong.

She chose a setting, a country house in a small Essex village, and a method, poison, and, most importantly, invented a detective, a retired Belgian policeman by the name of Hercule Poirot. With the necessary ingredients in place she set to work and wrote steadily until, about halfway through, she became stuck. Following family suggestions, she took herself off to a remote hotel in the middle of Dartmoor and immersed herself in her writing, finishing the manuscript within a fortnight in the summer of 1916.

Her husband, home on leave, enjoyed the story, entitled *The Mysterious Affair at Styles,* and recommended that the manuscript be submitted to Methuen where a friend of his was a director. But Methuen sat on the novel for six months before rejecting it, and another publisher was approached with a similar result. Christie sent her manuscript to yet a third publisher, The Bodley Head, where it languished.

However, other events in her life conspired to make her forget about her hopes of publication. Her husband, now a colonel, was posted to the Air Ministry, and they set up home in a small flat in London. Later, following the birth of their daughter Rosalind in 1919, they moved to a larger flat in London, and Archie Christie, released from his wartime job following the cessation of hostilities, obtained a post in the City. Then, nearly two years later, Christie received a letter from John Lane, the Managing Director, inviting her to call and see him. At the meeting, Lane told the excited young author that he was prepared to publish *Styles* if she made certain changes to it. Christie was so delighted that she signed what turned out to be a very tough contract. Nevertheless, she was on her way. A legend had begun.

The 1920s

Above: Abney Hall at Cheadle near Stockport, set in 350 acres of land, was the country mansion of the Watts family. The house was built in 1847 for the Mayor of Manchester, Sir James Watts, who was the youngest partner in the family business. Soon afterwards Watts set in motion building work to enlarge the house and decorate the interiors lavishly. He commissioned Pugin, architect of the Houses of Parliament, to design the interiors, but Pugin died in 1852 and the famous interior designer J. G. Crace, notable for his beautiful wallpapers, completed the house's transformation between 1852 and 1857. The interior today still has the heavy gothic influence of Pugin. Watts bought much of the furniture at the Crystal Palace Exhibition, and this completed the distinctive appearance. By 1900 his son, James Watts the younger, had inherited and enlarged the house again, and his son, another James, then met and married Marjorie Miller, whose mother had known James Watts' mother. Madge, as she was known, came from a comfortably-off American family living in Torquay, Devon, and was the elder sister of Agatha, later Christie. Agatha and Madge would spend many evenings composing and putting on plays and writing stories. Abney became Agatha's greatest inspiration for country-house life, with all the servants and grandeur which have been woven into her plots. The descriptions of the fictional Styles, Chimneys, Stonygates and other houses in her stories are mostly Abney in various forms.

Right: London society fashions, 1916.

14 • The 1920s

THE MYSTERIOUS AFFAIR AT STYLES

New York: Dodd, Mead, 1920; London: The Bodley Head, 1921

Background

Christie started writing *The Mysterious Affair at Styles* in 1916. As she later described in her autobiography, she began the process methodically. Given her experience, poison was an obvious choice of murder method. To use it effectively, the murderer needed close and familiar access to the victim or victims and, to confuse the reader, there had to be several candidates all operating in the same closed community with the opportunity to commit the crime.

Left: Ladies' tennis, a leisure sport for country living, in 1916.

Christie then had to decide the background, character and methodology of her detective. She had been an avid reader of Arthur Conan Doyle's detective stories but decided that her detective should be as different as possible from Sherlock Holmes, if only to escape the inevitable charge of imitation. However, the device of using a comfortable and sympathetic figure who was privy to the thought processes of the great detective and to whom the average reader could relate was irresistible, and so Captain Hastings, Poirot's Dr Watson, was born.

Her detective had to have a profession, but what was it to be? He could not be a scientist-detective like Holmes or a priest-detective like Chesterton's Father Brown. He could not be a serving policeman because that would require extensive knowledge of police procedures, which Christie did not have. She recalled that there were Belgian refugees living in Torquay and decided that her detective should be a retired Belgian policeman, a past which would allow him to have extensive experience of solving crimes but in a different professional milieu. Belgian nationality would guarantee Poirot sympathy from the reader, only too aware of what was happening just over the English Channel, but would also allow Christie to confer on him a distinctive style – not to say eccentricity of style – which might make him a figure of fun at times. In terms of physique and dress, even in choice of name, Hercule Poirot was born to be patronised by his Anglo-Saxon betters, until, inevitably, he showed his mettle and beat the plodding professionals at their own game by the exercise of those little grey cells with which he was so amply endowed.

BROMIDE OF POTASSIUM.

COX & ROBINSON,
Chemists,
STONY STRATFORD.

Left: A period label for potassium bromide, which, combined with strychnine, formed the fatal ingredient in the murder.

Opposite above: A village dispensary of the early 1900s.

Opposite below: The filming of *The Mysterious Affair at Styles,* by Carnival Films.

Storyline

As the story begins, Captain Arthur Hastings, the narrator, is staying in a dreary convalescent home having been invalided back home from the Western Front. A chance meeting with a boyhood acquaintance, one John Cavendish, results in an invitation to his home, which Hastings seizes with alacrity. At Styles Court, in Essex, Hastings re-establishes acquaintance with Cavendish's stepmother, now a redoubtable septuagenarian who rules the house with the proverbial rod of iron.

He also meets her new and much younger husband, Alfred Inglethorp, whom he describes as 'an absolute bounder'. When the old lady dies in a fit of convulsions, later determined to be the result of strychnine poisoning, suspicion naturally falls on her new husband. The country force calls in Scotland Yard in the person of Chief Inspector Japp, Christie's answer to Conan Doyle's Lestrade, who promptly arrests Inglethorp. In the meantime Hastings has met his old friend Hercule Poirot, late of the Belgian police, in the settlement for Belgian refugees set up in the nearby village by the late Mrs Inglethorp. Not confident that Inglethorp is the villain, he advises John Cavendish to let Poirot investigate the crime in parallel with the police.

There are other people at Styles too: Cavendish's wife Mary; his brother Lawrence; a young woman called Cynthia who works in the dispensary at the local hospital; an older woman called Evelyn Howard who was the secretary and companion of the old lady; and a mysterious foreigner called Bauerstein who is credited with being an expert on poisons and is recuperating from a nervous breakdown.

THE HAND IN THE DARK.

By ARTHUR J. REES, co-author of "The Hampstead Mystery," author of "The Shrieking Pit," etc. Crown 8vo. 9/- net.

A dinner party at a romantic old country house is in progress. Breaking in upon an interesting story by one of the guests comes a woman's piercing shriek, and a pistol shot from a room above. Panic among the guests; detectives sent for from far and near; suspicion darting like a poisoned arrow from one member of the household to another, and, after suspense and mental excitement, the unexpected conclusion comes as a surprise to the reader. This is no ordinary detective story—it has a literary quality and an atmosphere which give it an interest apart from the ingenious plot, and put it into the rare class of literary detective novels.

JOHN LANE,
The Bodley Head, W.1.

THE MOUNTEBANK. By W. J. LOCKE, Author of "The House of Baltazar," "The Rough Road," "The Beloved Vagabond," etc., etc. 7s. 6d. net.

THE DARK GERALDINE By J. A. FERGUSON, Author of "Stealthy Terror." 8s. 6d. net.

THE GUARDED ROOM By G. I. WHITHAM, Author of "Mr. Manley," "St. John of Honeylea," etc. 8s. 6d. net.

THE BREATHLESS MOMENT. By MURIEL HINE, Author of "The Hidden Valley," "Earth," "Autumn," etc. 8s.6d. net
"Amusing, well-told, always interesting, quite admirably constructed—in fact one of the few really interesting novels I have read this autumn season." (R. KING.)—*Tatler.*

THE DIPPERS. By BEN TRAVERS. 7s. 6d. net.
"A capital farce in which the absurdities are made really amusing. Mr. Ben Travers is a joker to be thankful for. . . . His audacity is justified by his humour."—*Daily Mail.*

THE HAND IN THE DARK. By ARTHUR J. REES, Author of "The Shrieking Pit," etc. 9s. net.
"I hasten to recommend 'The Hand in the Dark. . . . warranted to make a long journey pass like a flash, or a dull evening an occasion of tense excitement."—*Evening News.*

THE CONQUERING HERO. By JOHN MURRAY GIBBON, Author of "Hearts and Faces," etc. 8s. 6d. net.

THE LUCK OF THE MOUNTED. By RALPH S. KENDALL, Author of "Benton of the Royal Mounted." 7s. 6d. net.
"Sergeant Kendall writes about the Royal Canadian Mounted Police with inside knowledge. The background of snowy Canadian scenery, admirably painted in, lends a touch of poetry to the tale."—*Times Literary Supplement.*

THE TRUSTY SERVANT. By G. V. McFADDEN, Author of "The Honest Lawyer," etc. 10s. net.
"She again exhibits her power of re-creating the ideas, the languages, and the manners of a past generation. The tale   has a grip and a colour of its own that should give it some claim to a place among the Dorset classics."—*Scotsman.*

THE MYSTERIOUS AFFAIR AT STYLES. By AGATHA CHRISTIE. 7s. 6d. net.

THE IMPOSSIBLE APOLLO. By THOMAS COBB, Author of "The Dissemblers," "The Silver Bag," etc. 8s. 6d. net.

MY ORIENT PEARL. By CHARLES COLTON. 8s 6d. net.

JOHN LANE, THE BODLEY HEAD, VIGO ST., W.1.

THE MYSTERIOUS AFFAIR AT STYLES

AGATHA CHRISTIE

THE BODLEY HEAD

Christie gives the reader a great deal of help in the form of plans of the layout of the first floor of the house and of the victim's bedroom together with examples of handwriting, letters, mysterious messages and so on, in addition to the carefully developed plot, but as like as not, most readers will not know the solution until the neat little foreign detective, with his egg-shaped head, waxed moustaches and quaint command of the English language, solves the murder – to the amazement and discomfiture of the police and everyone else.

Above: The first UK edition of *The Mysterious Affair at Styles*, published in January 1921 following serialization in the *Weekly Times*. The American edition preceded it, published in December 1920. The role of dust-jackets in selling fiction was only just beginning to be realized at this time, as detective stories were swiftly developing the huge popular market they have today. The Bodley Head designed their wrappers in creamy white with other authors promoted on the back cover, with an enticing lead-in for the new novel on the front flap. As far as the authors are aware, this is the only early Bodley Head title not to have the price of 7 shillings and 6 pence marked on the spine as well as the front flap. We would welcome any further information from collectors.

Top left: The first UK edition of the novel, published in January 1921.

Top right: 'Styles', Sunningdale, Surrey, the house Agatha and Archie Christie bought in the mid 1920s. Named by them after her first novel, it already had a history of bad luck and they were not happy there.

Bottom right: An unusual shape of poison bottle from the Edwardian period.

Bottom left: A strychnine bottle from the Edwardian period, still unopened today. Agatha learnt much about all kinds of drugs and their effects. A senior chemist alarmed her when he described the sense of power he felt when handling curare, a lethal poison which she used in *Death in the Clouds*. Her knowledge of drugs was considerable and her suspects often took all manner of sleeping draughts.

Book Description

The book is a standard demy-octavo volume bound in brown cloth with decoration and lettering in black on the upper cover and spine. The volume, like *Poirot Investigates*, is slightly taller than the other four Bodley Head Christies, at 194 mm by 125 mm. The volume consists of 296 pages, of which the text runs from pages 9 to 296; there are no advertisement leaves. The very detailed dust-wrapper design by Alfred James Dewey faithfully reproduces the moment when the house party discovers the dying Mrs Inglethorp.

Reviews

In an interesting if slightly sour review, R. Cecil Owen, writing in the *Pharmaceutical Journal* of 7 May 1921, takes Christie to task over the chemistry of the strychnine cocktail and also over the reprimand handed out by the Coroner to the local pharmacist, who apparently supplied a quantity of strychnine to the local squire, having observed the legal requirements. The review concludes with the double-edged observation, 'The enlightened reader will observe that [the book] ranks high as a work of fiction, every care having been taken to keep as far away from the truth as possible.'

But when the 1923 reissue was reviewed in the same journal, the unnamed reviewer struck a more positive note: 'This novel has the rare merit of being correctly written – so well done in fact, that we are tempted to believe either that the author had a pharmaceutical training or had called in a capable pharmacist to help her over the technical part. In any case, the pharmacist reader's susceptibilities are not offended at any stage of the story.'

Spin-Offs

The Mysterious Affair at Styles, starring David Suchet as Poirot, was first shown on London Weekend Television on 16 September 1990. A still from the production is shown here.

THE SECRET ADVERSARY

London: The Bodley Head, 1922; New York: Dodd, Mead, 1922

Background and Storyline

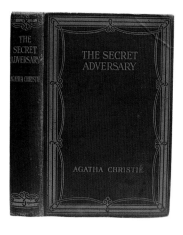

Right: The first UK edition, bound in dark blue-green cloth with a stylish art-nouveau border design.

Christie's second book was not a detective story but a thriller. John Lane, her publisher, was disappointed by this and at one point threatened to reject the manuscript, but was persuaded that it could be profitable. After being serialized in the *Weekly Times*, like its predecessor, the book went on to sell quite well. *The Secret Adversary* introduced Tommy and Tuppence, more formally Thomas Beresford and Prudence Cowley, who were to appear in four more books: *Partners in Crime* (1929); *N or M?* (1941); *By the Pricking of My Thumbs* (1968) and *Postern of Fate* (1974), by the last of which the dynamic duo had become an ageing married couple with grandchildren.

The first adventure begins when old friends Tommy and Tuppence meet up in London shortly after the end of the First World War. Well connected and with time on their hands following demobilization, they decide to go into business together as the 'Young Adventurers'. They are recruited by a Mr Carter of the British Secret Service and asked to recover secret papers which had been entrusted to a young woman called Jane Finn, last seen queuing for a lifeboat on the sinking *Lusitania*. Publication of the documents could seriously embarrass the British government and their recovery is vital. Suspicion has fallen on a mysterious character known as Mr Brown, 'the master criminal of this age' and the man behind the Bolshevik agitation which is feeding labour unrest in the country and inciting Sinn Fein across the water.

Tommy and Tuppence have to contend with a variety of interesting characters, including Julius P. Hersheimmer, Jane Finn's American millionaire cousin; Albert the lift-boy in a block of flats in Mayfair (who is to become a long-term employee of the Beresfords); and Sir James Peel Edgerton KC, a lawyer tipped as a future prime minister. The book ends with the unmasking of Mr Brown, the averting of a general strike and the growing awareness that our hero and heroine have stronger feelings for each other than they had thought.

In 1928, the German-language edition of *The Secret Adversary* was made into a film, *Die Abenteuer Gmbh* [Adventures Ltd], which picks up on the first chapter, 'The Young Adventurers Ltd', an early projected title for the book. The film, one of the last silent movies, was directed by Julius Hagen and starred Carlo Aldini and Eve Gray. In 1983, *The Secret Adversary,* the first of a ten-episode series based on the adventures of Tommy and Tuppence, was made for television, starring James Warwick and Francesca Annis.

Above: The first-edition dust-jacket, which now shows the UK price on the spine, with the same components used for *The Mysterious Affair at Styles.*

Book Description

The book measures 190 by 120 mm. It is bound in dark-green cloth with lettering and decoration in light green and consists of text pages 9 to 312 plus four pages of advertisements. The dust-wrapper is mainly typographical: the inner flaps promote *The Mysterious Affair at Styles* and the lower panel advertises other Bodley Head titles. The upper panel is pictorial with a dramatic design in black, red and white.

THE MURDER ON THE LINKS

London: The Bodley Head, 1923; New York: Dodd, Mead, 1923

Background

Christie completed most of the work on *The Murder on the Links* before accompanying her husband on a promotional tour for the projected British Empire Exhibition, which took them to South Africa, Australia, New Zealand and Canada via Fiji and Honolulu. Her publishers were delighted with the book but Christie was less enthusiastic about the finished product, taking the publishers to task over the design and colours of the dust-wrapper, to which she had taken an instant and strong dislike. She accepted the finished artwork on this occasion but secured an agreement that in future her approval would be needed.

In addition to her spat with her publishers (one of a number which suggest a slightly tense relationship), Christie also had a problem with one of her own characters, Captain Hastings. In her autobiography, she confessed, 'I thought I might as well marry off Hastings. Truth to tell, I think I was getting a little tired of him. I might be stuck with Poirot, but no need to be stuck with Hastings too.' Her irritation with a character of her own making is perhaps understandable but just as Conan Doyle had stuck with Watson, Christie was to find Poirot and Hastings more difficult to separate than she had anticipated.

Storyline

The idea for the story came from a lurid newspaper report of a murder in France, in which masked men had broken into a hotel, killing the owner and leaving the wife bound and gagged. Inconsistencies in the wife's account suggested that she might have colluded or even that she was the murderer herself.

As the novel begins, Poirot receives a letter from a man called Paul Renauld, who is in fear of his life and asks the detective to attend him urgently. Poirot and Hastings lose no time but when they arrive at the man's villa in Northern France they discover their prospective client has been murdered. Poirot learns that the servants had discovered the front door ajar and Renauld's wife tied up and gagged, and his body had been found stabbed, lying in an open grave on the edge of the neighbouring golf course.

Opposite right:
The set interior of the villa designed and built by Rob Harris and Carlotta Barrow for the LWT dramatization.

Left: Fashions of 1922, the year before *The Murder on the Links* was published. Egyptian designs were all the rage, with the recent discovery of Tutankhamun's tombs by Lord Carnavon and his team. Later in the decade Agatha would become increasingly interested in the excavations of Leonard and Katherine Woolley.

The Murder on the Links • 25

THE MURDER ON THE LINKS

Right: The first UK edition of *The Murder on the Links*, bound in a very attractive peach cloth with the art-nouveau linear design now characteristic of The Bodley Head.

Far right: The first UK dust-wrapper for *The Murder on the Links* with a section at actual size. Christie had a dispute with the publishers about the design and insisted that all future designs be approved by her.

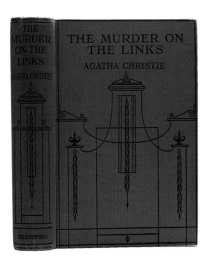

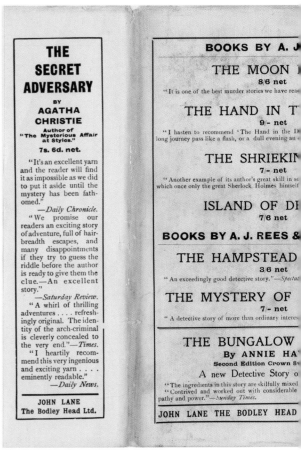

As ever, the clues and possible suspects pile up. There is a will just two weeks old; a love letter from a woman called Bella; a late-night visit from a Madame Daubreuil; a fragment of a torn-up cheque with the name Duveen on it; the identification of the murder weapon by Madame Renauld as a present from her son who has just left for South America on an urgent mission for his father; and the reporting of threats to the murdered man by a man speaking Latin-American Spanish.

Quite early in the proceedings, Inspector Giraud of the Surêté arrives and makes clear that Poirot's presence is unwelcome. A series of encounters between Poirot and Giraud ensues, culminating in a wager by Poirot that he will identify the murderer before Giraud. Then there is a second murder. Hastings meets Poirot off the Paris train to give him the news. Poirot is initially staggered but he then proceeds to describe the second murder, to Hastings' astonishment. Later Poirot confides the results of his visit to Paris. He has managed to identify one of the major characters as a key participant in a murder trial twenty years before, in which there were important similarities with the present case. After some breathtaking but entirely logical exercises of the

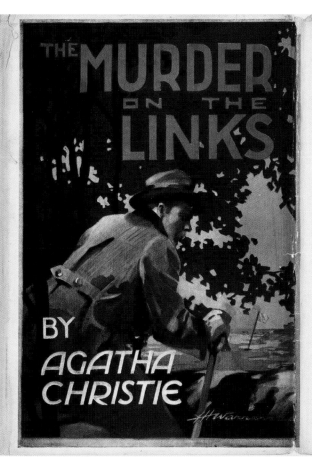

Opposite: Filming *The Murder on the Links* with David Suchet and Hugh Fraser in the lead roles of Poirot and Hastings.

famous grey cells, Poirot identifies the murderer, wins his wager with Giraud and also secures Hastings a wife. Happily for the reader, Christie relented and decided not to pension Hastings off, having concluded reluctantly that Poirot without Hastings would be like Holmes without Watson.

Book Description

The book is a standard demy-octavo, 190 mm by 125 mm. The first edition is dated on the title verso, 'First published in 1923', in capitals. The text begins on page 9 and finishes on page 319. It is followed by eight pages of advertisements for other Bodley Head titles, including Christie's first two books. The book is bound in orange cloth with lettering and decoration in black on the upper cover and spine.

Reviews

The book was the recipient of rave reviews, typical of which was the following, taken from the *Evening News*: 'A wonderful triumph. It is with congratulations to Miss Christie and to the large contingent of admirers of the detective novel that I make the announcement that in this writer there is a distinguished addition to the list of writers in this genus.' In the *British Weekly*, 'Man of Kent' wrote, 'It will rejoice the heart of all who truly relish detective stories … the feat was amazing. The book is put together so deftly that I can remember no recent book of the kind which approaches it in merit. It is well written, well proportioned, and full of surprises. Lovers of good stories will, without exception, rejoice in this book.'

Spin-Offs

The Murder on the Links, starring David Suchet as Poirot, was adapted for television by London Weekend Television and first shown on 11 February 1996.

THE MAN IN THE BROWN SUIT

London: The Bodley Head, 1924; New York: Dodd, Mead, 1924

Background and Storyline

The dust-wrapper follows the pattern of the other Bodley Head Christies. It is basically typographical but most of the upper panel is given over to a rather feeble pictorial representation of the early scene in which Anne Beddingfield, the heroine, witnesses the death of a man who falls onto the track at Hyde Park Corner underground station and is electrocuted. The body is recovered and a tall man in a brown suit claiming to be a doctor proceeds to examine it. He leaves in a hurry, dropping a piece of paper which bears the words 17-22 Kilmorden Castle. Our heroine suspects that the death is not accidental and persuades a newspaper owner, who is reminiscent of the contemporary press magnate Lord Northcliffe, to fund her investigation.

Another death, this time at the home of Sir Eustace Pedler MP, leads Anne to take ship to South Africa. On the *Kilmorden Castle* she makes the acquaintance of Sir Eustace and his sinister secretary – characters based in part on Major Belcher and his secretary, whom Christie and her husband had got to know on their tour of Africa. Pedler was not Belcher entire, Christie was later to write in her autobiography, 'but he used several of Belcher's phrases and told some of Belcher's stories. He too was a master of the art of bluff, and behind the bluff could easily be sensed an unscrupulous and interesting character'. The story, set mostly on board ship and in South Africa and Rhodesia, is told through the diaries of Anne and Sir Eustace. The villain of the piece is a man known as 'the colonel', to whom robbery, forgery, murder and espionage are meat and drink. Eventually, with a little help, our heroine unmasks the colonel and loose ends are all satisfactorily tied up. While Christie does not feature Anne again in any future story, the strong silent Colonel Race reappears in three later novels. Her publishers had hoped for a detective story but got instead a well-paced thriller with a strong sense of place, which aficionados consider one of her best. Reviews were generally enthusiastic, as exemplified by J. Franklin writing in the New Statesman, '*The Man in the Brown Suit* is the best of its kind I have met for a long time. It is remarkable especially for a brand new device for concealing the villain's identity to the very end. I defy the most practised hand to discover him.'

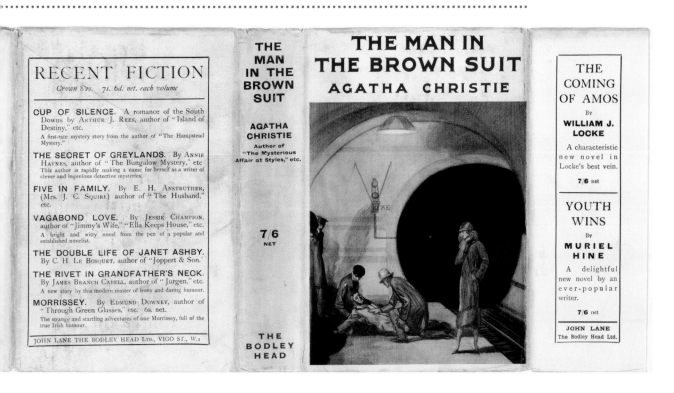

Book Description

The volume measures 190 mm by 125 mm and consists of 312 pages of which the text occupies pages 3 to 310; the last two pages consist of advertisements. It is bound in grey-brown cloth lettered and decorated in dark brown with the same pattern as used in *Poirot Investigates*.

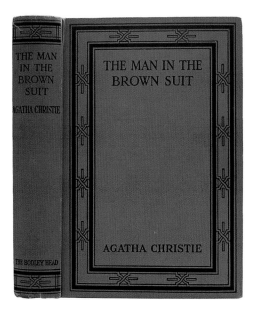

Above: The first UK edition dust-wrapper, in the established Bodley Head design format. The front cover is not considered to be a strong design, but this did not detract from any of Christie's sales.

Left: The UK cloth binding of *The Man in the Brown Suit,* with the characteristic art-nouveau pattern on the spine and front cover.

POIROT INVESTIGATES

London: The Bodley Head, 1924; New York: Dodd, Mead, 1924

Background

The origins of *Poirot Investigates* are to be found in a request to the author from Poirot fan Bruce Ingram, editor of *The Sketch*, for a series of short stories for his weekly illustrated magazine. Christie agreed with alacrity and the first of the series (originally consisting of eight stories, later extended, perhaps unwisely, to twelve) appeared in the issue of 7 March 1923 along with a page of photographs of the author at home. Christie approached The Bodley Head with the suggestion that the serialized stories be collected and published in book form as soon as possible to capitalize on the serialization and this was agreed. The collection was provisionally entitled *The Little Grey Cells of M. Poirot,* picking up on a caption used in the serialization, but this was dropped in favour of the shorter title. The UK edition consisted of only eleven stories while the American edition contained fourteen. British readers who might have thought themselves short-changed had to wait fifty years for the missing three stories to be published in *Poirot's Early Cases,* although one of the three stories, 'The Veiled Lady', was published in 1946 with two different short stories in the slim volume *Poirot Lends a Hand.*

Above: This large handsome art-deco house was used for the filming of 'The Disappearance of Mr Davenheim', one of the stories in *Poirot Investigates*, by Carnival Films. A private property in Surrey called Joldwyns, it still has all its original fittings, notably the steel windows which are so vital to the period glamour. The art-deco movement was just about to burst onto the scene in Paris in 1925, after which it never looked back.

Storyline

The collection begins with 'The Adventure of The Western Star', which is a delightful pastiche of a Sherlock Holmes short story with Captain Hastings playing a particularly dim Watson to Poirot's Holmes. The story starts with Hastings totally misreading a street scene outside Poirot's apartment block which Poirot, with barely a glance, gets right. It concludes with Poirot humiliating Hastings by explaining how his friend had been so easily duped, and solving the mystery which involves a film star, members of the aristocracy and the diamond of the title and its putative mate, not to mention mysterious Chinamen.

The collection continues with an apparent suicide which Poirot, very dramatically, determines is murder. In the third story, chance remarks by Hastings about the fortuitous letting to acquaintances of a Knightsbridge flat at a

POIROT INVESTIGATES

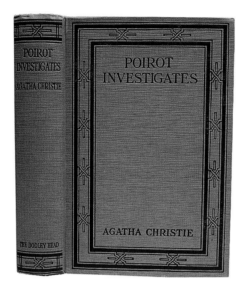

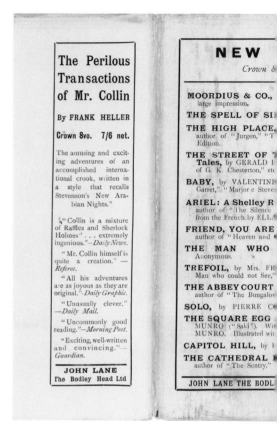

Above: The bright yellow cloth binding of the first edition, a colour that lasts extremely well, showing the customary Bodley Head motifs.

Right: The first UK dust-wrapper for *Poirot Investigates*. This black and white jacket, which appears rather plain at first glance, is a stark contrast to the bright yellow cloth book beneath it. Christie's previous successes are being promoted more strongly, here listed on the spine.

ridiculously low rent excite Poirot's curiosity and lead eventually to the recovery of stolen naval plans. In the following story, Hastings fills in for a Poirot brought low with flu and is allowed to investigate a suspicious death in a locked gun-room, provided he reports fully to Poirot each day and follows instructions to the letter. Needless to say, the investigation, which has also baffled Inspector Japp, is solved by Poirot from his sickbed.

The fifth story centres around the theft of bonds from a locked portmanteau on board an Atlantic liner bound for New York and their sale within half an hour of the ship's arrival. 'The Adventure of the Egyptian Tomb' involves Poirot and Hastings in the strange deaths of the archaeologists investigating

POIROT INVESTIGATES
BY
AGATHA CHRISTIE

(spine)

POIROT
INVESTIGATES

AGATHA
CHRISTIE

Author of
"The Mysterious Affair
at Styles,"
"The Murder on the Links,"
etc.

7/6
NET

**THE
BODLEY
HEAD**

(left flap)

...TION

7/6 *net*

...IAM J. LOCKE. Third

MURIEL HINE.

...ES BRANCH CABELL,
of the Jest," etc. Second

...E, and Nine other
author of "The Innocence

...E, author of "The Happy

..., by ANDRÉ MAUROIS,
Bramble," etc. Translated
[Second Edition.

... by ALICE HERBERT,
...oss," etc.

...R UNDERSTOOD.

...NOLDS, author of "The

...ER, by ANNIE HAYNES,

...T, author of "Sidonie."

...er Stories, by H. H.
...ir of "Saki" by E. M.
...sketches by "Saki."

...FERGUSSON.

...y NICOLAI LYESKOV,

LTD., VIGO ST., W.1

(right flap)

In the
Mayor's
Parlour

By J. S. FLETCHER

*Popular Crown 8vo.
Edition, 3/6 net*

"A detective story in
the author's very best
manner." — *Morning
Post.*

"A skilfully construct-
ed mystery." — *Daily
Mail.*

"One of the best
sensation stories that
Mr. Fletcher has given
us." — *Westminster
Gazette.*

"An ingenious story."
—*Spectator.*

"One of the best of
Mr. Fletcher's stories."
—*New Statesman.*

JOHN LANE
The Bodley Head Ltd.

(spine)

POIROT
INVESTIGATES

AGATHA
CHRISTIE

Author of
"The Mysterious Affair
at Styles,"
"The Murder on the Links,"
etc.

POIROT INVESTIGATES
BY
AGATHA CHRISTIE

Above: A scene from the TV drama of 'The Jewel Robbery at the Grand Metropolitan'; the scene does not appear in the story but was added for dramatic effect. Sorcha Cusack takes the lead role.

the opening of an ancient Egyptian tomb, in a manner reminiscent of the deaths following the opening of Tutankhamn's tomb by Lord Carnarvon. Poirot works it out 'in spite of la mer maudite, the heat abominable, and the annoyances of the sand'.

Of the remaining stories, among which figure a jewel robbery by the sea, the disappearance of a banker, a phone call from a dying man and the mystery of the missing will, quite possibly the best is 'The Kidnapped Prime Minister'. It is possible to see some of the political views expressed by some of the characters as those of the author herself but perhaps more interesting is the description Poirot provides of his methodology.

At a tense moment, when Poirot is expected to leap into a military car to pursue the action, he refuses to leave Boulogne and retires to a private room in a nearby hotel where he explains his actions to the assembled company: "'It is not so that the good detective should act, eh? I perceive your thought. He must be full of energy. He must rush to and fro. He should prostrate himself on the dusty road and seek the marks of tyres through a little glass. He must gather up the cigarette-end, the fallen match? That is your idea, is it not?" His eyes challenged us. "But I – Hercule Poirot – tell you that it is not so! The true clues are within – here!" He tapped his forehead. "See you, I need not have left London. It would have been sufficient for me to sit quietly in my rooms there. All that matters is the little grey cells within. Secretly and silently they do their part, until suddenly I call for a map, and I lay my finger on a spot – so – and I say: the Prime Minister is there! And it is so! With method and logic one can accomplish anything!"'

Book Description

The book is a demy-octavo, marginally taller than the previous three. It is 198 mm by 128 mm, with text pages 1 to 298 plus 14 pages of advertisements. It is bound in a yellow cloth with decorations and lettering in dark blue. The black and white wrapper has on its upper panel a splendid portrait of Poirot by W. Smithson Broadhead; the detective is complete with egg-shaped head and waxed moustache, and immaculately turned out with hat and cane, spats and pointed patent-leather shoes. The spine shows the price of 7/6.

Spin-Offs

All fourteen stories were adapted for television and starred David Suchet as Poirot. They were first transmitted on London Weekend Television between 1990 and 1993.

The same year Geoffrey Bles published *The Road of Dreams*, a collection of poems by Christie written over several years. The first section, 'A Masque from Italy', contains nine poems to be performed by characters from the *commedia dell' arte*, a theme later developed in the Harley Quin stories. There is also an interesting poem called 'In the Dispensary' which includes the splendid lines, 'Here is menace and murder and sudden death! – in these phials of green and blue!'

Clockwise from top left: Abney Hall, with all the grandeur that Christie describes in the book; a beautiful stained-glass window on the ground floor; fashions of 1925, of the type that sleuth Lady Eileen 'Bundle' Brent might have worn; the grounds of Abney Hall, illustrating the elegant landscape.

THE SECRET OF CHIMNEYS

London: The Bodley Head, 1925; New York: Dodd, Mead, 1925

Above: The gothic-style bannisters of the interior at Abney Hall.

Background

The Secret of Chimneys was the last Christie novel to be published by The Bodley Head, appearing in June 1925. Christie was grateful to John Lane for getting her career as a writer under way but not so grateful, thanks principally to the onerous nature of the initial contract, that she wished to remain with them, however tempting the terms and conditions of any subsequent contract. *Chimneys* famously includes a jibe by one character about another character's book to the effect that it would be at least a year before it was published because publishers sat on manuscripts and hatched them like eggs. However gentle a dig, it suggests at least one ground for dissatisfaction with her publishers. Indeed, Christie was so unhappy with The Bodley Head that her literary agent had secured a new contract for her before her obligations to her first publisher had been fulfilled. Collins were to be her new publishers and she was to remain with them until her death.

The Christies had been wanting to leave London for some time and they moved first to a mansion flat in a large Victorian house at Sunningdale in Berkshire, conveniently near to the Sunningdale Golf Club, which Archie joined. Having decided they liked the neighbourhood (which for Archie meant the golf club and relative proximity to London), they moved into their own house with a large garden in 1925 and named it Styles after the house in Christie's first novel.

Storyline

Reckoned by her critics to be one of the best of Christie's early thrillers, *Chimneys* is a light-hearted tale free from the self-imposed plot complexities of many of her books. The story concerns itself with politics in the fictitious Balkan state of Herzoslovakia but is set in London and at Chimneys, a country house which is based physically on Abney Hall, the Victorian pile inherited by the Watts, in-laws of Christie's older sister Madge, and frequently visited by the author, but whose style and setting are more reminiscent of Cliveden, home of the Astors.

Books by Agatha Christie

THE SECRET ADVERSARY

Second Edition.
Crown 8vo. 3/6 net

"It's an excellent yarn and the reader will find it as impossible as we did to put it aside until the mystery has been fathomed."—*Daily Chronicle.*

THE MURDER ON THE LINKS

Fourth Edition.
Crown 8vo.
7/6 net and 3/6 net

"One of the best mystery stories I have read."—S. P. B. MAIS in *The Daily Express.*

"A clinking yarn, most ingeniously contrived and skilfully evolved . . . there is not a superfluous word or a dull one from start to finish . . . the very best of this sort of fiction."—WINIFRED BLATCHFORD in *The Clarion.*

JOHN LANE
The Bodley Head Ltd.

NEW FICTION. 7s. 6d. *net*

THE SECRET ROAD. By John Ferguson, author of "Stealthy Terror," "The Dark Geraldine," etc.
A capital mystery story of an unusual kind, written in the powerful and distinguished style which has gained Mr. Ferguson his reputation.

MISCHIEF. By Ben Travers, author of "The Dippers," "A Cuckoo in the Nest" and "Rookery Nook." Third Edition.
'From start to finish this delightful comedy is handled with unflagging wit and ingenuity.'—*Times Lit. Supp.*

THE BLUE DIAMOND. By Annie Haynes, author of "The Bungalow Mystery," "The Secret of Greylands," etc.
A thrilling new mystery story, full of excitement and suspense.

WHY THE SPHINX SMILES. By Ethel Knight Kelly.
A powerful study of human emotion and human frailty.

PROFESSOR, HOW COULD YOU! By Harry Leon Wilson, author of "Ruggles of Red Gap," "Oh, Doctor!" etc.
The story of a little hen-pecked professor who suddenly runs away and has the wildest adventures, most amusingly told by this popular writer—the best thing of its kind since O. Henry's "Gentle Grafter."

BULLWHACK JOE: The Yarns of a Tenderfoot. By R. B. Townshend, author of "A Tenderfoot in Colorado," and "The Tenderfoot in New Mexico."
Racy stories of pioneer days in Colorado, full of movement and incident.

THE SPICE OF LIFE. By Olive Gregory.
This is a first novel of unusual quality, warm-blooded and buoyant, with a plot which is neither exotic nor hackneyed, easy natural dialogue and a wide popular appeal.

THE LITTLE BROWN BABY. By Peter Blundell, author of "The Finger of Mr. Blee," "Love Birds in the Coconuts," etc.
An amusing farcical story of the East, full of gusto and fun, by a well-known writer.

JOHN LANE THE BODLEY HEAD LIMITED, VIGO ST., W. 1.

Above: The first UK dust-wrapper for *The Secret of Chimneys.* The depiction of armour derives from the heavy Victorian design of Abney Hall's interior, and also from Marple Hall, which also had a sumptuous decor filled with armour and impressed Agatha at this time. Marple Hall, now demolished, provided the name for her most famous amateur sleuth, Miss Marple. This vintage of jacket and book would sell for over £15,000 today. Each year the asking prices are continually rising and buyers compete fiercely at auctions.

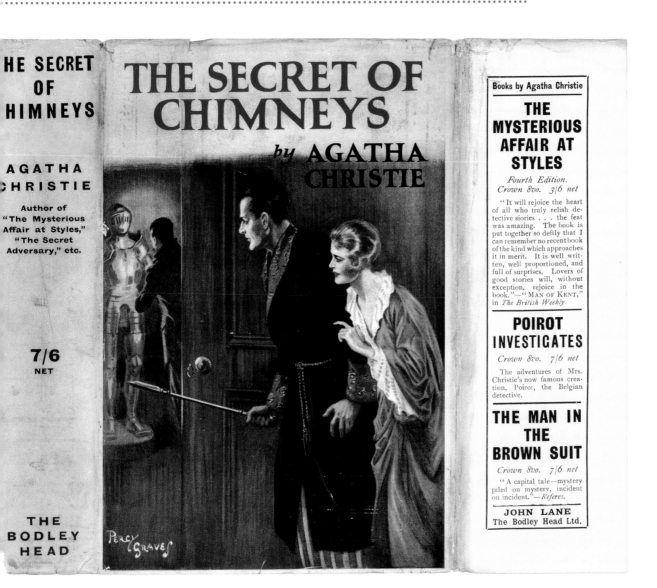

Two plot-lines are ingeniously combined: the possible restoration of the Herzoslovakian royal family, the subject of much diplomatic intrigue, and the activities of an international jewel thief known as King Victor. In addition to Lord Caterham, the ninth Marquess and owner of Chimneys, characters include his daughter 'Bundle', more formally called Lady Eileen Brent, who is destined to play an important part; her sisters Daisy and Dulcie; Prince

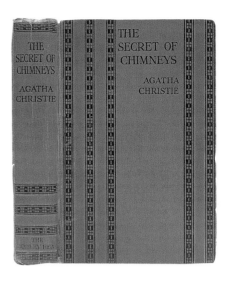

Clockwise from top left: The interior of Abney Hall, showing its glittering vibrant gothic decor. This staircase also inspired the setting for *Dumb Witness* and *Sleeping Murder*; the first UK edition, bound in a beautiful sky blue, with a vertical patterning to the boards; the lake in the grounds at Abney Hall, the inspiration for Chimneys in the novel.

Michael Obolovitch, whom the British government hope will become King of Herzoslovakia and who is visiting Chimneys for discussions with Lord Caterham; Baron Lolopretjzyl, the London-based representative of the Loyalist Party of Herzoslovakia, who lives in a suite at Harridge's Hotel and has serious difficulties with English word order; one Anthony Cade, who has come to England from Bulawayo to return love-letters to a woman called Virginia Revel, who is apparently being blackmailed, and to deliver the memoirs of Count Stylptich which may contain revelations important for the future of Herzoslovakia; the Honourable George Lomax, a particularly pompous politician and the bane of Caterham's life; Herman Isaacstein, a financier of Middle Eastern antecedents, about whom Christie, through her characters, makes remarks which would not be permitted in today's more enlightened climate; Bill Eversleigh, Lomax's secretary, an amiable if vacuous young man who has strayed in from a Wodehouse novel; and Prince Michael's decidedly scary valet.

A murder is committed and Colonel Melrose, the Chief Constable, calls in Superintendent Battle of Scotland Yard, who is far removed from Christie's usual policemen, who tend not to be renowned for their intellectual and professional prowess and have to be rescued by the likes of Poirot and Marple. Battle, who is to appear in four more Christie stories, is well up to the task of investigating two shootings, blackmail and the matter of a fabulous missing jewel. By application of intelligence and dogged determination he succeeds in bringing matters to a successful conclusion, which involves a startling denouement.

Book Description

The book is a standard demy-octavo volume, measuring 190 mm by 120 mm, with text pages 1 to 306 plus two pages of advertisements. It is bound in light-blue cloth decorated and lettered in black.

Reviews

The reviews were generally favourable. The *Times Literary Supplement* referred to 'a thick fog of mystery, cross purposes, and romance, which leads up to a most unexpected and highly satisfactory ending'. The *Literary Review* commented, 'Here's another capital detective story ... which will keep the reader guessing until the very end, not only as to the identity of the arch villain – the murderer – but also that of the hero.'

THE MURDER OF ROGER ACKROYD

London: Collins, 1926; New York: Dodd, Mead, 1926

Background

Above: A candlestick-type telephone in working order from the 1920s.

This novel was the first to be published in the UK by Collins, with whom Christie was to remain to the end. It appeared in the spring of 1926 and was to prove in many respects a breakthrough work. It established Christie as a formidable new talent within the genre; was to be her first big seller (a first printing of a mere 5000 copies or so notwithstanding) and generated a debate that continues to this day about what constitutes fair play in reaching a solution which is properly accessible to the reader.

The Detection Club, an association of crime writers of which Christie was a member, which existed to foster interest in the genre and also to maintain high standards, had laid down rules about the use of evidence, which Christie was deemed to have broken. Writers, critics and readers were divided. But support

Flora Ackroyd.

"M. Porrett."

Above left: Flora Ackroyd as conceived in the newspaper serializations, in which the audacious plot was revealed to avid readers.

Above centre: Poirot's country suit for the modern production, designed by Charlotte Holdich. The green tweedy material was intended to provide an image of a dapper Poirot in the country, growing vegetable marrows.

Above right: An early impression of Hercule Poirot, known by characters in the book as 'M. Porrett'.

for Christie came from her fellow novelists. The formidable Dorothy L. Sayers rose to her rival's defence by making the point that 'it is the reader's business to suspect everyone'. Julian Symons, crime writer and critic, also defended Christie, describing the denouement as 'the blandest, most brilliant of deceptions'.

No less a personage than Lord Mountbatten is credited with having provided Christie with the controversial plot-line; many years later Christie sent him a copy of *Ackroyd* with a handwritten inscription thanking him for 'the suggestion which I subsequently used in … Ackroyd'. Mountbatten was certainly convinced that the idea was his, but other research suggests that Christie's own brother-in-law, James Watts, was responsible. Neither man incidentally was favoured by the book's dedication, which was 'To Punkie [Christie's sister Madge] who likes an orthodox detective story, murder, inquest, and suspicion falling on everyone in turn!' Whoever was responsible, and it is by no means impossible that both men could claim credit for the idea, Christie used it to devastating effect.

Storyline

The story takes place in a characteristically charming and sleepy English village called King's Abbot. It begins with the death of Mrs Ferrars, a wealthy widow. The local doctor, Sheppard, who is the narrator, believes it may be suicide but keeps his views to himself. The very next day, Roger Ackroyd, a wealthy widower whom the locals had linked romantically to the dead woman, is found dead in his study. By a remarkable coincidence Sheppard's neighbour is one Hercule Poirot, retired and vegetating. It is not long before he is assisting the slow-witted local police in their investigations, with Sheppard as his aide. In classic style, attention focuses on one character after another, each of whom has the motive and/or the opportunity to have committed the murder. Major Blunt, an old friend and big-game hunter, seems keen on Flora, the murdered man's niece; Flora and her mother, Ackroyd's widowed sister-in-law, are both without means and dependent on Ackroyd, and Ackroyd's secretary, Geoffrey Raymond, seems to have harboured resentment against his late employer. Then there is an adopted son, Ralph Paton, who has gambling debts and finally Ursula Bourne, a parlourmaid who is not what she seems. Needless to say, Poirot eventually succeeds in solving the two deaths, with the help of Sheppard and the doctor's sister and housekeeper, Caroline, a nosy middle-aged spinster who is in some respects the prototype of Miss Marple. The occasional infelicity apart, the characters and background are wholly convincing and the reader is well set up for the startling denouement.

Book Description

The book is a standard demy-octavo. The text block measures 183 mm by 122 mm and it consists of 320 pages, numbered from 1 to 312. It is bound in dark-blue cloth, lettered in red on the spine and upper cover, which displays the author's name and book title in upper-case letters within a double red border. The spine also has two red rules at the extremities. Copies bound in light-blue cloth lettered in black are later issues. The dust-wrapper artwork was done by Ellen Edwards. The design, picturing a rather furtive-looking Mrs Ackroyd searching the drawers of her late brother-in-law's desk for his will, is very similar in style to those done for two other crime thrillers published by Collins: G. D. H. & M. Cole's *The Death of a Millionaire* (1925) and J. Kilmeny Keith's *The Man Who Was London* (1925). The artwork is insipid and undistinguished and so it is perhaps unsurprising that the publishers turned to other artists for Christie's later works.

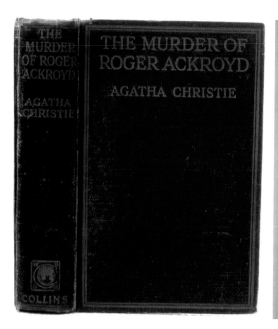

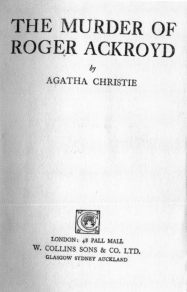

THE MURDER OF ROGER ACKROYD

by

AGATHA CHRISTIE

LONDON: 48 PALL MALL
W. COLLINS SONS & CO. LTD.
GLASGOW SYDNEY AUCKLAND

Clockwise from top left: The first UK edition, bound in navy cloth by Collins, showing the red ruled line surrounding and adjacent to the title pages; the title page of the first UK edition; ladies' fashions of 1926, here a warm coat and hat, with heavy fur cuffs and collar; the motive for the murder: a recreation of the letter written on the distinctive blue letter-paper by Mrs Ferrars to Roger Ackroyd, confessing her crime and her blackmailer; the discovery of the body, an illustration from the early newspaper serialization.

We staggered into the room and saw Ackroyd dead in his armchair in front of the fire.

THE MURDER OF ROGER ACKROYD

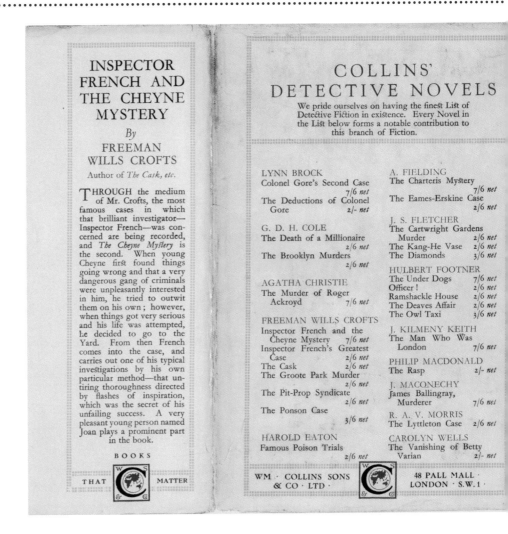

Reviews

Opinion at the time was, as it still is, divided. The *Daily Sketch* thought the book 'the best thriller ever'; the *News Chronicle* however dismissed it as 'a tasteless and unfortunate let-down by a writer we had grown to admire'. One reader was so outraged by the denouement that he wrote a letter to the editor of *The Times* declaring that he was now a former admirer and would not be buying any more of the author's books. Christie herself remained unmoved, convinced that while it would have been wrong for an author to have lied to

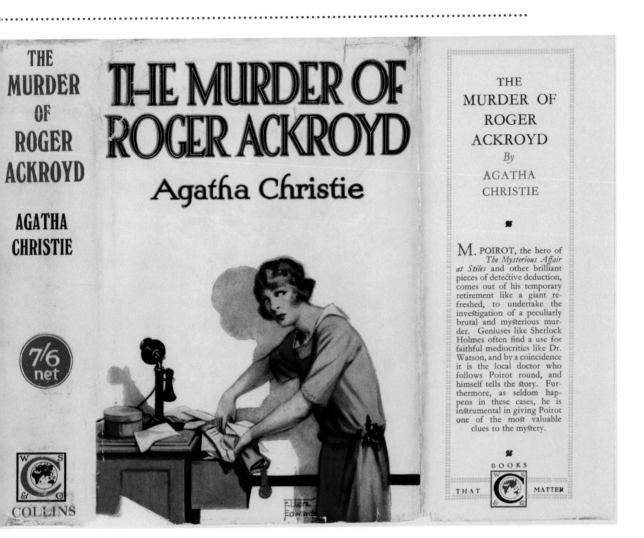

Above: The first-edition dust-jacket of *The Murder of Roger Ackroyd*, which shows the Collins logo of the day with other well-known writers' promotions on the rear cover. The storyline as advertised on the front flap gives no hint of the startling ending. Many dust-jackets of this time were printed on white paper, which of course is unforgiving to wear and tear. The jacket does not really reflect the novel's importance. However none of these observations would have any impact on the desirability of this book for modern collectors.

the reader, it was not unreasonable to be economical with explanation. The book was to remain one of her favourites. Whatever the pros and cons of the debate, the furore had an effect on her sales which was overall entirely beneficial for the author.

Spin-Offs

In 1928, Michael Morton adapted *Ackroyd* for the stage, with the title *Alibi*. He was to take some liberties, of which Christie strongly disapproved, but was persuaded to abandon the more outrageous – which included knocking some twenty years off Poirot's age, calling him Beau Poirot and having girls falling for him all over the place. Christie, with great reluctance, allowed Morton to reduce the age of Caroline Sheppard in order to provide Poirot with a love interest. Her feelings are understandable because the character of Caroline Sheppard and her place in the village were vital to the original story (and anticipate the arrival of the formidable Miss Marple) and it was important to the development of Poirot that he, like Sherlock Holmes, should remain single and unattached, with a male interlocutor in the person of Arthur Hastings. The play opened at the Prince of Wales Theatre on 15 May 1928 with a distinguished cast including Charles Laughton as a competent Poirot (if totally unlike Christie's own conception). It was a commercial success, running for 250 performances in the West End. Renamed *The Fatal Alibi,* it opened in New York in 1932 with Laughton directing and starring but closed after a mere twenty-four performances.

In 1931, the play was turned into a film, retaining the title *Alibi*. Produced by Julius Hagen who had already filmed *The Secret Adversary*, it was shot at the Twickenham Studios, with Austin Trevor as even less Poirot-like than Laughton. Audiences had to wait until 2000 for a superb film performance of *Ackroyd* with David Suchet as the definitive Poirot in the Carnival Films LWT series.

THE BIG FOUR

London: Collins, 1927; New York: Dodd, Mead, 1927

The book was written at a difficult time for Christie. The year had begun with the death of her mother and was followed by the collapse of her marriage, which led her to the verge of a nervous breakdown. An indication of the degree of the trauma is contained in a letter to her publishers in which she proposed a change of name. But they insisted that her public had become used to her as Agatha Christie and she accepted this with considerable reluctance. Written when she was desperate for money, the novel is a rewriting of twelve Poirot short stories first published in *The Sketch*. The Big Four – a Chinese man, an American, a French woman and an Englishman known as 'the destroyer' – constitute an international crime syndicate which Poirot destroys with help from Hastings, Inspector Japp and his brother Achille.

The volume measures 190 mm by 120 mm and consists of 288 pages. It is bound in dark-blue cloth, lettered in red on the spine and upper cover and with a double red border on the upper cover and double red rules to the spine extremities. The upper panel of the UK dust-wrapper features London in silhouette, with the title overprinted, surmounted by a huge figure four, partially overprinted by the author's name.

Below: The first US dust-jacket, eagerly promoting *The Murder of Roger Ackroyd* and *The Big Four.*

The Big Four • 51

THE MYSTERY OF THE BLUE TRAIN

London: Collins, 1928; New York: Dodd, Mead, 1928

Background and Storyline

This was another novel written whilst Christie was recovering from the breakdown of her marriage. She was later to say that she hated it and thought it the worst she had written. Her readers did not agree and while it is far from her best book, it is not a bad read. It is based on her short story 'The Plymouth Express', later published in the UK in *Poirot's Early Cases* (1974) and in the USA as one of eight stories in *The Under Dog* (1951). Poirot, travelling without Hastings on this occasion, is drawn into the story by virtue of being on the same luxurious train (the domestic equivalent of the Orient Express and operated by the same company) as the murdered woman, Ruth Kettering, an American millionaire's daughter whose marriage is in difficulties and who just happens to be carrying the fabled Heart of Fire ruby, en route for the French Riviera. Poirot's little grey cells are brought to bear with formidable effect.

In addition to the beautifully described Riviera, part of the story is set in the village of St Mary Mead in which an elderly lady called Miss Viner with impressive powers of observation, a prototype of Miss Marple, plays a small part. Despite Christie's unhappy memories of the story, the reviews were generally favourable. The *Times Literary Supplement* commented, 'The reader will not be disappointed when the distinguished Belgian on psychological grounds … builds up inferences almost out of the air, supports them by a masterly array of negative evidence and lands his fish to the surprise of everyone.'

Book Description

The volume measures 190 mm by 130 mm and consists of 304 pages; the collation is viii, 1-295 with no advertisement leaves. It is bound in dark-blue cloth with red lettering on the upper cover and spine. There is a red border to the upper cover and red rules at the spine extremities. The spine also contains the Collins logo, repeated on the title page, which was soon to be replaced by the Crime Club gunman. The dust-wrapper is basically typographical with an upper panel featuring two gendarmes leaning over a dead female body and the unmistakable head and shoulders of Poirot beaming down from the spine.

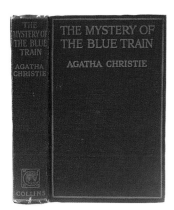

Above: The first UK edition dust-wrapper is energetic in design, with wonderful artwork illustrating the unfolding drama. Poirot now has an established visual persona, which is not unlike many of the more successful later attempts to capture the essence of his character.

Left: The UK cloth-bound first edition of *The Mystery of the Blue Train*.

THE SEVEN DIALS MYSTERY

London: Collins, 1929; New York: Dodd, Mead, 1929

Opposite above:
The UK dust-
jacket, featuring
clock-dial head-
wear. This is one
of the hardest-to-
find jackets, with
delightful period
graphic artwork
and typeface.

Opposite below:
Country-house
dress of 1929.
such as the hero-
ine 'Bundle'
would have worn.

Background and Storyline

The Seven Dials Mystery is a sequel to *The Secret of Chimneys*. It features the same setting and many of the characters, including Colonel Melrose, Chief Constable; Superintendent Battle of Scotland Yard; Lord Caterham, the owner of Chimneys; and Lady Eileen 'Bundle' Brent. Chimneys has been rented to a family called the Cootes, but one of their house guests, the notoriously late riser, Gerry Wade, fails to wake up despite the noise made by seven alarm-clocks placed on his mantelpiece by mischievous friends. The cause of death is poisoning.

A second house guest, Ronny Devereux, meets the same end, but not before telling Bundle about the significance of the Seven Dials. This leads her, with the assistance of Jimmy Thesiger, a friend of the two dead men, to the Seven Dials Club, home of a sinister secret society whose members are hooded and address each other only by numbers. The mystery is eventually solved at Wyvern Abbey, home of Sir Oswald Coote, after the timely intervention of Superintendent Battle.

Book Description, Reviews and Spin-Offs

The UK edition is bound in black cloth, with red lettering on the front cover and spine. The boards measure 190 mm by 120 mm. Text runs from pages 1 to 276 plus six pages of advertisements.

Reviews were generally favourable, though the *New York Times* advised its readers that 'the author has been so keen on preventing the reader from guessing the solution that she has rather overstepped the bounds of what should be permitted to a writer of detective stories. She has held out information which the reader should have had'. It was a charge which had been made before and was to recur.

The book was dramatized to wide acclaim by London Weekend Television in 1981 with a stellar cast which included John Gielgud, Harry Andrews, Cheryl Campbell and James Warwick.

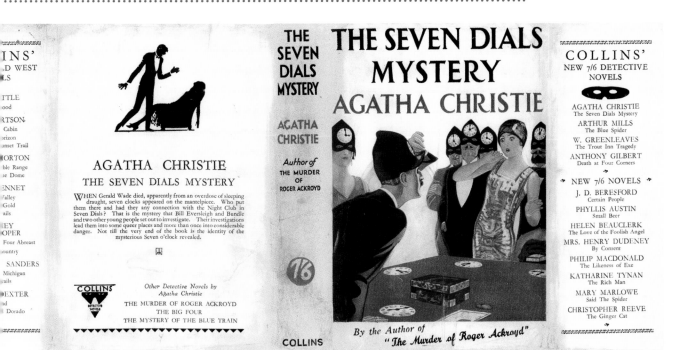

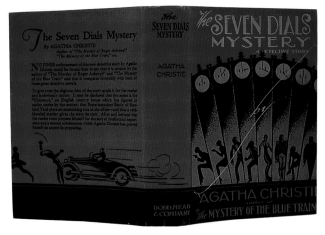

Above: The novel's first appearance in America resulted in a bright red graphic design with type-face and artwork as shown.

PARTNERS IN CRIME

London: Collins, 1929; New York: Dodd, Mead, 1929

....

Background and Storyline

Right: The first UK edition dust-wrapper of *Partners in Crime.* This is perhaps the most successful and typical example of 1920s jacket design, though the white background suffers heavily after seventy years. The title has stayed in the imagination of the crime-reading public ever since and is a much-used phrase today.

Tommy and Tuppence, now married, crave excitement. When Mr Carter, now head of the Secret Service, offers them an assignment, they accept immediately. Their brief is to run the International Detective Agency, which enables them to monitor the activities of the Bolsheviks and also to take on any other cases which may turn up. Tommy claims that he has read 'every detective novel that's been published in the last ten years', which allows Christie to show him tackling each case in the manner of a different fictional detective.

The Bolshevik threat surfaces periodically before being despatched in the last story, but the main focus of the book is to provide Christie with an opportunity to parody her contemporary writers of detective fiction, which she does superbly. The characters assumed by Tommy include Sherlock Holmes, Father Brown, Inspector Hanaud and Hercule Poirot himself, alongside others who have not all stood the test of time. The stories work brilliantly as parodies but are not otherwise of special merit. Chapters 11 to 22 were republished by Collins in paperback under the title *The Sunningdale Mystery.*

Book Description

The first UK edition measures 192 mm by 125 mm and consists of 256 pages of which the text occupies pages 7 to 251. The last three leaves promote 'New 7/6 Detective Novels'. It is bound in black cloth lettered in red on the upper cover and spine, with a single red border on the upper cover and a single red rule at each spine extremity. The dust-wrapper is mainly typographical but with a pictorial upper panel in red, blue, black and white, which features Tommy and Tuppence in evening dress accompanied by a bloodhound against a window lit by a full moon. Tuppence brandishes a magnifying glass and Tommy a gun, while a malevolent humanoid shadow hangs over him.

COLLINS'
NEW 7/6 FICTION

ROSE MACAULAY
Staying with Relations
MRS. ALFRED SIDGWICK
Six of Them
PHYLLIS BOTTOME
Windle Straws
REGINALD BERKELEY
The Lady with a Lamp
VICTOR L. WHITECHURCH
First and Last
FLORENCE KILPATRICK
Hetty's Son
FRANK ROMER
The Playful Double
E. WYNNE TYSON
Melody
NORMAN GILES
Keerboskloof
KATHARINE HAVILAND
TAYLOR
Pablito
KATHARINE TYNAN
The River
LADY TROUBRIDGE
That Great Vow
HOLLOWAY HORN
The Intruder

....

PARTNERS
IN CRIME

THIS delightfully witty book will come as a pleasant
surprise to all admirers of these ingenious detective
thrillers for which Agatha Christie is famous. It tells the
story of the amazing adventures of two amateur detectives—
Tommy, a remarkable young man of thirty-two, and his
equally remarkable wife, Tuppence—who follow the methods
of famous detective heroes, such as Sherlock Holmes, Inspector
French, Roger Sheringham, Bulldog Drummond, Father
Brown and even Monsieur Poirot himself. Problem after
problem comes before them for solution, and the account
of their endeavours to live up to their slogan, " Blunt's
Brilliant Detectives ! Any case solved in twenty-four hours ! "
makes delicious reading.

Versatile
AGATHA
CHRISTIE
Writer of Thrills

EXCELLENT RECENT NOVELS BY THIS CLEVER
author include

THE SEVEN DIALS MYSTERY
THE MURDER OF ROGER ACKROYD
THE MYSTERY OF THE BLUE TRAIN

PARTNERS
IN CRIME

AGATHA
CHRISTIE
AUTHOR OF
THE SEVEN DIALS
MYSTERY
etc

7/6
NET

Returning
at
2.30 A M

COLLINS

AGATHA CHRISTIE

PARTNERS *in* CRIME

COLLINS'
NEW 7/6 DETECTIVE
NOVELS
AGATHA CHRISTIE
Partners in Crime
FREEMAN
WILLS CROFTS
The Box-Office Murders
ROBERT GORE-BROWNE
Death on Delivery
LYNN BROCK
The Mendip Mystery
A. FIELDING
Let Furnished
HULBERT FOOTNER
The Doctor Who Held Hands
ARTHUR MILLS
Pursued
FRANCIS D. GRIERSON
The Yellow Rat
JOHN STEPHEN STRANGE
The Clue of the Second Murder
J. JEFFERSON FARJEON
The 5.18 Mystery
WILLIAM GAVINE
Wings of Mystery
VERNON LODER
The Vase Mystery
RALPH RODD
Blind Man's Buff
A. C. AND CARMEN
EDINGTON
The Studio Murder Mystery
VIRGIL MARKHAM
Shock !

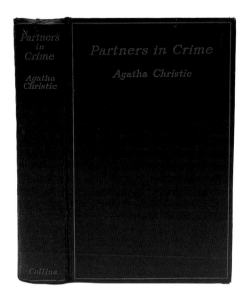

Left: Fashionable travelling clothes of the mid to late 1920s, suitable for lady sleuths!

Far left: The UK cloth binding of *Partners in Crime.*

Partners in Crime • 57

IMPERIAL AIRWAYS

EUROPE·AFRICA·ASIA·AUSTRALIA

The 1930s

THE MYSTERIOUS MR QUIN

London: Collins, 1930; New York: Dodd, Mead, 1930

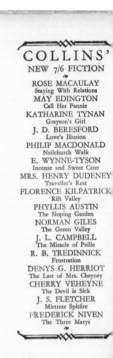

Background and Storyline

The book contains twelve short stories featuring Mr Quin and Mr Satterthwaite, all first published in magazines during the 1920s. Two Mr Quin stories are not included in this collection 'The Harlequin Tea Set', written in the 1950s, eventually appeared as a contribution to *Winters Tales 3*, an anthology published in 1971, and 'The Love Detectives', originally published in *Flynn's Weekly* in 1926, first appeared in book form in the UK in *Problem at Pollensa Bay* (1991), though it was published in the USA in 1950 in *Three Blind Mice*. Christie retained a special affection for these stories, which combined detection with the supernatural. She had refused to commit herself to producing a series of Harley Quin stories for any one magazine because it would have meant producing them to order, and for these stories she needed to feel appropriately inspired. The detection work was usually carried out by Mr Satterthwaite, 'a little bent dried-up man with a peering face oddly elf-like, and an intense and inordinate interest in other people's lives', but only after he had been inspired by the appearance of the mysterious Harley Quin, a self-appointed patron saint of lovers, who showed himself to his alter ego when a crime was committed which threatened to destroy the happiness of lovers. Satterthwaite without Quin seems a rather pathetic figure who lives life vicariously, but inspired by Quin the magician he is able to solve problems in a dramatic fashion that contrasts vividly with Poirot's application of his little grey cells.

Book Description

The UK first edition measures 190 mm by 125 mm and consists of 287 pages. The book is bound in black cloth lettered in red on the spine and the upper cover which has a single red ruled border. The dust-wrapper is mainly typographical but has a pictorial upper cover and spine with yellow lettering on a pale-blue background, with a smiling black-masked Harlequin figure with white shirt and black tie and diamond-patterned hose on the upper cover and a black and white Harlequin bust on the spine.

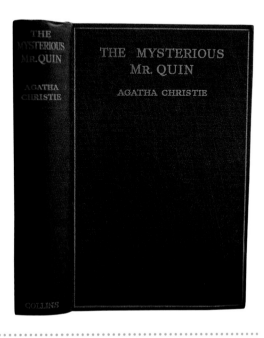

The Mysterious Mr Quin • 61

THE MURDER AT THE VICARAGE

London: Collins, The Crime Club, 1930; New York: Dodd, Mead, 1930

Background

1930 saw two momentous events in Christie's life: her happy marriage to Max Mallowan, an archaeologist fourteen years her junior whom she met on a dig in the Middle East, and the publication of her first novel to feature Miss Jane Marple, who was to become the world's best-known female sleuth.

From the point of view of her biographers Christie was unusually unhelpful about the genesis of this title. In her autobiography she is disarmingly vague, telling her readers that she could not remember how or where she came to write the book. It's hard not to suspect that Christie was bored with Poirot, not necessarily terminally, but sufficiently to inspire her to create an alternative sleuth. Whatever the reason for Miss Marple's introduction, Christie went on to remark that 'she had no intention of continuing her for the rest of my life' or letting her 'become a rival to Hercule Poirot', famous last words.

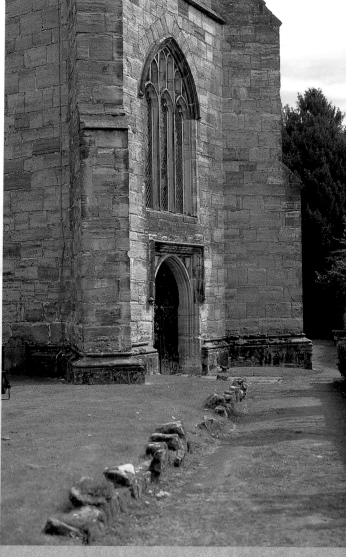

Above left: Country fashions of 1931, of the sort Lettice Protheroe, daughter of the first victim, could have worn. Here photographed at a vicarage in Berkshire, everyday clothing could be rugged but good-quality woollen tweeds, of sensible length. For smarter occasions, stylish dresses with a regular flower pattern and a gentle waist were now becoming fashionable, as styles moved away from the harsh lines of the 1920s and femininity came back into vogue. 1930 was a turning point and from here on, curves are back.

Above right: Penshurst village church; the grounds of any churchyard provide many unobtrusive paths for the suspect.

Opposite: Of the many hundreds of quintessential villages that the reader may have in mind when reading this novel, Penshurst in Kent fits Agatha Christie's requirements better than most. It has all the necessary ingredients: a large mansion, a church within feet of its vicarage (pictured); a post office, a telephone box, beautiful landscape, two pubs and a railway station about half a mile away. It still conveys the old-world charm that Christie describes. Georgian houses line the high street and were it not for the modern cars and street accessories it would make a suitable and attractive location for filming. Nearby Chiddingstone has been used for many period dramas.

Christie later admitted that the prototype for Miss Marple was Caroline Sheppard, the middle-aged spinster and sister-housekeeper of Dr Sheppard, the narrator of *Roger Ackroyd*. Christie's favourite character in the book, Caroline was an acute observer and intelligent listener who missed nothing that was happening in her village of St Mary Mead (another contrast to the metropolitan Poirot) and had the ability to apply what she had learned to solve problems that baffled the professionals.

Christie made Jane Marple older than Caroline Sheppard, a bit of a gossip, kind but shrewd and, above all, someone who always succeeded where others, usually the police, failed. The name Marple, Christie later admitted to members of the real Marple family, came from their family home, Marple Hall, which was not far from her sister's home at Abney Hall. At an estate sale at Marple Hall she purchased two Jacobean chairs which she was to keep for the rest of her life. Altogether, there were to be twelve full-length Miss Marple stories compared to thirty-three Poirot novels, which might suggest that the forces of the marketplace proved stronger than Christie's own predilections.

Right: Vicarage fashions of 1931. Agatha's new husband, Max Mallowan, would keenly enquire in letters from his archaeological digs how 'Protheroe' (the victim in *The Murder at the Vicarage*) was progressing.

Storyline

The story centres on local churchwarden and magistrate Colonel Lucius Protheroe, who is so thoroughly unpleasant that even the vicar of St Mary Mead, Leonard Clement, is driven to remark to his wife that 'anyone who murdered Colonel Protheroe would be doing the world at large a service'. When the Colonel is found murdered at the vicarage where he had an appointment with the vicar, who was called away on a false errand, it quickly becomes clear that there is no shortage of suspects. Miss Marple, whose home just happens to be next to the vicarage, is quickly in on the case. Officially, the murder is investigated by the rude and overbearing Inspector Slack, who has to contend with a surfeit of suspects – including the late Colonel's unfaithful

Left: Churston church was Agatha's nearest place of worship when she came to live at Greenway House on the banks of the River Dart in Devon; getting to it involved a walk and sometimes a train ride on the Dartmouth steam service. Churston made a famous appearance in *The ABC Murders* in 1936.

Below: An aerial view of the Devon villages illustrating all the beauties of English rural life.

A MASTER DETECTIVE NOVEL

SUGGESTED TO YOU BY THE CRIME CLUB PANEL

Exhilarating thrills . . . as good as a holiday . . . better than a play . . . right in your own favourite armchair . . .as regular as the clock. Before publication the good news comes in The Crime Club Bulletin . . . you merely order from your Library or Bookseller . . . and the book is yours to enjoy on publication day.

Return this Coupon. Your Membership commences immediately.

- -

THE CRIME CLUB OFFICES,

48 Pall Mall, London, S.W. 1.

Please enrol me right away as a Member of
THE CRIME CLUB.

I understand that no obligation or payment of any kind is attached to Membership.

Name,.....................................
(PLEASE WRITE IN BLOCK LETTERS)

Address,...............................

....

You may obtain the selected books from your Library in the usual way, or buy them as you feel disposed, on publication day.

THE CRIME CLUB

THE Crime Club has been formed so that all interested in Detective Fiction may, at NO COST TO THEMSELVES, be kept advised of the best new Detective Novels before they are published.   It costs you NOTHING TO JOIN THE CRIME CLUB.

DETECTIVE Novels are read by Cabinet Ministers, Business Magna Harley Street Specialists, Famous Judges, Bishops and Leaders of Relig Teachers, and men and women in every sphere of life, because there nothing so fascinating as a baffling crime problem, nothing so exhilarati so entertaining, so thrilling. Nothing so lifts a man or woman from cares and worries of present-day life.

THE Crime Club Jury consisting of well known connoisseurs of Detect Fiction will choose at regular intervals, the " Selected Book from The Crime Club List, which can be obtained from y usual bookseller or from your Circulating Library. AT NO TII WILL THE CRIME CLUB ENDEAVOUR TO SELL BOO THEMSELVES. THE SOLE AND ONLY OBJECT OF THE CRI CLUB IS TO HELP ITS MEMBERS BY SUGGESTING THE BE AND MOST ENTERTAINING DETECTIVE NOVELS OF T DAY.

YOUR BOOKSELLER IS YOUR LOCAL AGENT

Entry Form on Flap

JOIN NOW

ADVANTAGES OF MEMBERSHIP

Immediately your application reaches Crime C Headquarters your name is entered in the Direct of Members.

About 14 days in advance of publication you advised of the Crime Club Panel's selected boc

This information comes to you in the CRIME CL BULLETIN which also contains news of forthcom Crime Club publications, enabling you to obtain, publication day, the latest and best detective nov through your local bookseller or circulating library

Simplicity itself ! The experts confer, eliminate suggest to you the very best. You benefit by gua teed enjoyment, exclusive reading and the knowle that The Crime Club never lets its members down

IT COSTS YOU NOTHING TO JO

Above: The first edition of the jacket for *The Murder at the Vicarage*. This is a real delight for any artistic eye. Three typefaces are in evidence with the front flap carrying the Ashley Crawford type, for the title. There is a different linear design on the front and a slightly earlier style on the spine, with the first appearance of the display face Basuto on the rear cover and flap, which continued to be used for many years in various parts of the designs of all Collins Crime Club publications. This jacket is one of the hardest to obtain today in any condition.

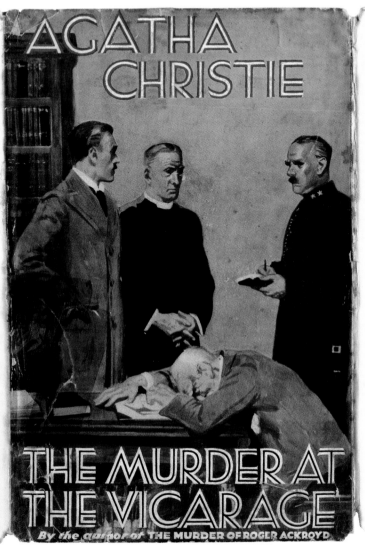

THE
MURDER
AT THE
VICARAGE

AGATHA
CHRISTIE
Author of
THE MURDER OF
ROGER ACKROYD etc.

7/6
NET

THE
CRIME
CLUB

THE MURDER AT THE VICARAGE

by

AGATHA CHRISTIE

IN the peaceful village of St. Mary Mead nothing ever happens. So it seems almost incredible when Colonel Protheroe, the churchwarden, is discovered, shot through the head, in the Vicarage study. Everybody thinks they know who has done it—including Miss Marple, the real old maid of the village who knows everything and sees everything and hears everything! She declares that at least *seven* people have reasons for wishing Colonel Protheroe out of the way! Excitement dies down when somebody confesses to having committed the crime. But that is not the end, for almost immediately somebody quite different also confesses! And there is a third confession through the telephone! But who *really* killed Colonel Protheroe?

Read also
THE ESSEX MURDERS
by VERNON LODER

MURDER TO MUSIC
by A. C. & CARMEN EDINGTON

wife and her lover Lawrence Redding, acting together or separately; Lettice Protheroe, the daughter who was due to inherit; and the local poacher, Bill Archer. Needless to say, Slack is soon way out of his depth and it is left to Miss Marple, whom Slack has treated with contempt, to disentangle the labyrinthine plot and devise the trap which will expose the killer. It is a triumphant debut for Miss Marple and arguably one of the best of the Marple stories.

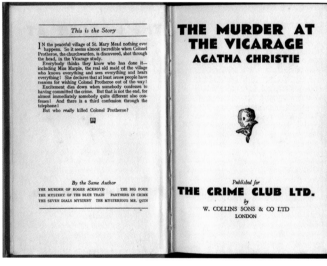

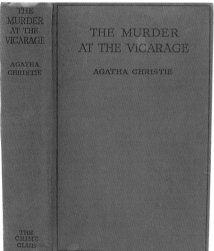

Top: The US jacket for *The Murder at the Vicarage* uses the gothic theme of the church for inspiration.

Above: The title pages and the first UK edition, cloth bound in orange. The title pages show the Basuto typeface in full use inside for the first time.

Right: Giant's Bread first-edition jacket with a Braque influence on the design.

Book Description

This was the first book to appear under Collins' new Crime Club imprint. It is a standard demy-octavo bound in red cloth, lettered in black. It consists of 256 pages of which the text runs from pages 7 to 254, with two pages of advertisements at the end.

Reviews

The reviews were mixed. 'Any book by Agatha Christie attracts attention but when she really hits her stride in a full length detective story, as she does in *The Murder at the Vicarage*, she is hard to surpass,' wrote their reviewer in the *Saturday Review of Literature*. On the other hand, Bruce Rae, writing in the *New York Times,* found that 'The talented Miss Christie is far from being at her best in her latest mystery story. It will add little to her eminence in the field of detective fiction.'

Spin-Offs

Adapted by Moie Charles and Barbara Toy, *The Murder at the Vicarage* opened at the London Playhouse on December 14 1949, produced by and starring Reginald Tate, and ran for five years, a measure of the praise it received from the critics and the paying public. The play was successfully revived in 1975 with Barbara Mullen as Miss Marple. In 1988, the novel was memorably televised with a very strong cast including Joan Hickson as Jane Marple, whose performance has to be considered definitive in this and other televisations of the Marple stories.

Giant's Bread

London: Collins, 1930. This was Christie's first novel as 'Mary Westmacott' and was followed by five others. That Westmacott and Christie were one and the same was a well-guarded secret until revealed in 1949 in the *Sunday Times*. The Westmacott novels are very readable but unlike Christie's detective stories add little to the genre. *Giant's Bread,* at 438 pages long, demonstrates appropriate depth of character and an impressive knowledge of its setting, the world of classical music.

THE SITTAFORD MYSTERY

The Sittaford Mystery, London: Collins, The Crime Club, 1931
Murder at Hazelmoor, New York: Dodd, Mead, 1932

Background and Storyline

Opposite above: The lively dust-jacket for the UK edition of *The Sittaford Mystery,* with the Basuto typeface in full use together with more traditional styles.

This novel is set in Christie's native Devon and her portrayal of the looming menace of Dartmoor in winter and its snow-bound inhabitants is masterly. The moor is not merely a setting but an additional personality and – in a twist reminiscent of *The Hound of the Baskervilles* – an escaped prisoner adds an additional frisson. As the story opens, the death of Captain Trevelyan is foretold in a séance and rapidly comes to pass. The tale continues with the arrest of the late Captain's nephew and with the efforts of his fiancée, Emily Trefusis, to find the real murderer. She does with the help of the local police who, in the absence of Poirot and Miss Marple, are obliged to be on their mettle.

Book Description

The volume measures 190 mm by 130 mm and consists of 256 pages of which the text occupies pages 9 to 250. The last three leaves advertise 'New 7/6 Detective Novels'. The book is bound in orange cloth lettered in black on the upper cover and spine. The dust-wrapper has promotional material on the inner flaps and on the lower panel, which advertises The Crime Club. The upper panel and spine are pictorial and feature two of the participants in the séance with which the book opens. The title of the US edition features the name of the house where the death occurs, while the UK title uses the name of the village and prefers to draw attention to the detection element rather than the nature of the crime.

Opposite right: The mint UK cloth edition, with the familiar Basuto embossed titles. The name Sittaford came from Sittaford Tor, on Dartmoor, where Christie completed her first book, *The Mysterious Affair at Styles,* after a visit to the Moorland Hotel.

Opposite far right: The US jacket is stylish and simpler than the British. The title was altered to the less significant name of Hazelmoor.

THE CRIME CLUB

HE Crime Club has been formed
so that all interested in Detective
ion may, at NO COST TO
EMSELVES, be kept advised of
best new Detective Novels before
are published. It costs you
THING TO JOIN THE
IME CLUB.

TECTIVE Novels are read by Cabinet Ministers, Business Magnates,
Harley Street Specialists, Famous Judges, Bishops and Leaders of
gion, Teachers, and men and women in every sphere of life, because
e is nothing so fascinating as a baffling crime problem, nothing so
arating, so entertaining, so thrilling. Nothing so lifts a man or
man from the cares and worries of present-day life.

HE Crime Club Jury, consisting of well known connoisseurs of
Detective Fiction, will choose at regular intervals, the "Selected
ks" from The Crime Club List, which can be obtained from your
l bookseller or from your Circulating Library. AT NO TIME
LL THE CRIME CLUB ENDEAVOUR TO SELL BOOKS
EMSELVES. THE SOLE AND ONLY OBJECT OF THE CRIME
B IS TO HELP ITS MEMBERS BY SUGGESTING THE BEST
D MOST ENTERTAINING DETECTIVE NOVELS OF THE
Y.

ADVANTAGES OF MEMBERSHIP

¶ Immediately your application reaches Crime Club Headquarters your name is entered in the Directory of Members.

¶ About 14 days in advance of publication you are advised of the Crime Club Panel's selected book.

¶ This information comes to you in the CRIME CLUB BULLETIN which also contains news of forthcoming Crime Club publications, enabling you to obtain, on publication day, the latest and best detective novels, through your local bookseller or circulating library.

¶ Simplicity itself! The experts confer, eliminate and suggest to you the very best. You benefit by guaranteed enjoyment, exclusive reading and the knowledge that The Crime Club never lets its members down.

UR
OKSELLER
YOUR
CAL
ENT

Entry Form on Flap

JOIN NOW

IT COSTS YOU NOTHING TO JOIN

THE
SITTAFORD
MYSTERY

AGATHA
CHRISTIE

AGATHA
CHRISTIE

Author of
THE MURDER OF
ROGER ACKROYD

7/6 NET

THE CRIME CLUB

THE SITTAFORD MYSTERY

THE SITTAFORD MYSTERY

By
AGATHA CHRISTIE

IT was a typical Dickens Christmas: deep snow everywhere, and down in the little village of Sittaford on the fringe of Dartmoor, probably deeper than anywhere. Mrs. Willett, the winter tenant in Captain Trevelyan's country house, was, with her daughter Violet, giving a party. Finally they decided to do a little table rapping and after the usual number of inconsequential messages from the "other side," suddenly the table announced that Captain Trevelyan was dead. His oldest friend, Captain Burnaby, was disturbed. He quickly left the house and tramped ten miles of snowy roads to Exhampton. There was no sign of life in Trevelyan's house. A back window was broken in and the light was burning—and there, on the floor, was the body of Trevelyan. Inspector Narracott took the case in hand, and after wandering through a maze of false clues and suspects, he ultimately discovered the murderer of Captain Trevelyan. Mrs. Christie has never formulated a more ingenious or enthralling plot and her characterisation is of the vivid type which marked *The Murder at the Vicarage* and *The Murder of Roger Ackroyd*.

Read also
THE WRAITH
by PHILIP MACDONALD

HUE AND CRY
by BRUCE HAMILTON

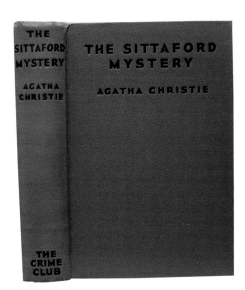

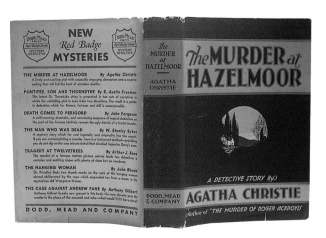

Top: An aerial view of the River Dart.

Right: Southsands, near Salcombe, provided a perfect setting for the very stylish production filmed in 1990. Here one can see the Victorian house that represented End House, home of the Buckley family in the novel and based on Abney Hall, home of Agatha's brother-in-law James Watts. The name Buckley was shared in real life by connections of the Watts.

PERIL AT END HOUSE

London: Collins, The Crime Club, 1932; New York: Dodd, Mead, 1932

Background

1932 proved to be another productive year for Christie. Building on the excellent reception afforded her first Miss Marple novel, *The Murder at the Vicarage,* she followed up with six short stories featuring Miss Marple for a magazine, collected in book form as *The Thirteen Problems,* and with *Peril at End House,* a full-length story starring Poirot, Hastings and Japp. Writing in her autobiography thirty years on, Christie asserted, '*Peril at End House* was another of my books that left so little impression on my mind that I cannot even remember writing it.' But despite the author's modesty, Christie aficionados reckon it to be one of her best books, with an ingenious plot and stronger characterization than is the case in some of her stories.

Below: An aerial view of the coast of Devon, close to where Agatha Christie grew up in Torquay. She later came back to the area to live at Greenway, on the banks of the River Dart.

Peril at End House • 73

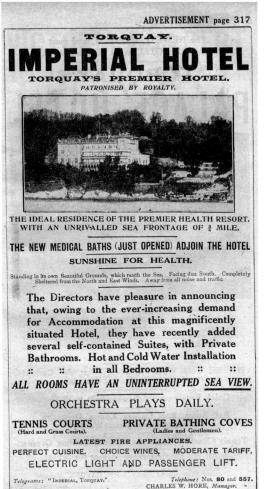

TORQUAY.

IMPERIAL HOTEL

TORQUAY'S PREMIER HOTEL.

PATRONISED BY ROYALTY.

THE IDEAL RESIDENCE OF THE PREMIER HEALTH RESORT.
WITH AN UNRIVALLED SEA FRONTAGE OF $\frac{3}{4}$ MILE.

THE NEW MEDICAL BATHS (JUST OPENED) ADJOIN THE HOTEL

SUNSHINE FOR HEALTH.

Standing in its own Beautiful Grounds, which reach the Sea. Facing due South. Completely Sheltered from the North and East Winds. Away from all noise and traffic.

The Directors have pleasure in announcing that, owing to the ever-increasing demand for Accommodation at this magnificently situated Hotel, they have recently added several self-contained Suites, with Private Bathrooms. Hot and Cold Water Installation :: :: in all Bedrooms. :: ::

ALL ROOMS HAVE AN UNINTERRUPTED SEA VIEW.

ORCHESTRA PLAYS DAILY.

TENNIS COURTS
(Hard and Grass Courts).

PRIVATE BATHING COVES
(Ladies and Gentlemen).

LATEST FIRE APPLIANCES.

PERFECT CUISINE. CHOICE WINES. MODERATE TARIFF.

ELECTRIC LIGHT AND PASSENGER LIFT.

Telegrams: "IMPERIAL, TORQUAY."

Telephone: Nos. **80** and **557.**
CHARLES W. HORE, *Manager.*

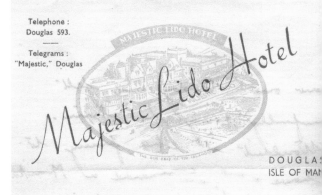

Telephone : Douglas 593.

Telegrams : "Majestic," Douglas

Majestic Lido Hotel

DOUGLAS
ISLE OF MAN

Clockwise from top left: An advertisement from *The ABC Railway Guide* for the Imperial Hotel, which is generally considered a likely model fictional Majestic hotel of St Loo in the plot; an elegant lady boating in 1932 – wearing trousers, a daring new fashion; an attractive letterhead of a Majestic Hotel in the 1930s.

Storyline

The story is set in the fictional resort of St Loo in Cornwall, although it is clear from the description that it is in fact a thinly disguised Torquay, with the fictional Hotel Majestic, at which Poirot and Hastings are staying for a few days, standing in for Torquay's grandest establishment, the Imperial.

While at the Majestic, Poirot and Hastings meet a delightful if enigmatic young woman called Nick Buckley who lives at End House, an imposing if slightly run-down house situated on the nearby cliffs in view of the hotel. In the course of conversation, it transpires that Miss Buckley has had three brushes with death in as many days. Poirot is convinced someone is trying to kill her, a suggestion which the young woman laughingly rejects until her cousin is killed at End House presumably mistaken by the murderer for Nick.

The lively collection of characters, mostly connections of the dashing heroine, includes a young Jewish art dealer called Jim Lazarus; an idiosyncratic couple, Bert and Millicent Croft, who are Australian to the point of caricature; the red-faced bluff Commander George Challenger who is in love with Nick; Charles Vyse, a local solicitor, Nick's cousin, and the heir to End House; and Frederica 'Freddie' Rice, Nick's chum who has been deserted by a deadbeat husband and longs to be free to marry Jim Lazarus.

Christie pulls the wool over the eyes of her readers in outrageous fashion, employing a clever plot device she enjoyed so much that she used it again. Poirot's little grey cells are on top form, and he solves the mystery with a little help from his old sparring partner Chief Inspector Japp – drafted in by the local force, who as usual admit defeat at the earliest opportunity.

Above left: Young girls in the latest fashions of 1931–2.

Below left: Embossed 1930s typeface for a Majestic Hotel in the Isle of Man, illustrating the block type in the art-deco style in a bright vermillion, a popular colour at that time.

Peril at End House • 75

PERIL AT END HOUSE

Above: The first cloth UK binding, here preserved in unusually mint condition beneath the matching jacket, shown alongside.

Right: The first UK edition of the jacket for *Peril at End House,* stunningly preserved in spite of the white background and spine, which usually suffer from the wear of seventy or more years of use. The front is not quite what one might expect, but it still has the unmistakable design of the art-deco movement and the variety of typefaces are always sumptuous to behold, with Basuto as usual. The Crime Club entice the reader to join them and *'Poirot returns'* is exclaimed with great dash and excitement.

Below right: A section at full size.

THE CREAM OF DETECTIVE FICTION

SELECTED FOR YOU BY THE **CRIME CLUB** PANEL

THE panel of five experts (including Dr. Alington, Headmaster of Eton) selects three detective stories per month and announces them to you, *free of all charge*, in the Quarterly *News*. The books are obtainable, on the First Monday in Every Month, at every bookshop and library.

RETURN COUPON BELOW
YOUR MEMBERSHIP BEGINS AT ONCE

TO THE
CRIME CLUB HEADQUARTERS, 48, PALL MALL, LONDON, S.W. 1

Please enrol me at once as a member. I understand that no payment or obligation of any kind is attached to membership.

NAME..

ADDRESS...
    PLEASE WRITE IN BLOCK LETTERS

....

....

AT EVERY BOOKSHOP AND LIBRARY

THE SIGN OF A GOOD CRIM

Have you joined

THE CRIME C

OVER 25,000 persons have joined a
The list includes doctors, clergymen, la
University Dons, civil servants, business
it includes two millionaires, three world-f
statesmen, thirty-two knights, eleven pee
the realm, two princes of royal blood ar
princess. . . . Why? Why this extraor
success in less than two years? *First*, bec
good crime novel is the finest recreation obta
at the price. Its problems intrigue you, its
exhilarate; you arise from it refreshed
invigorated, with your worries forgotten.
    because a bad crime novel only irrit
and exasperates. The Panel of five exper
selects the good and eliminates the
bad—*and its service is free.*

JOIN NOW!

IT COSTS YOU NOTHING

Have you joined

THE CRIME CLUB

OVER 25,000 persons have joined already.
The list includes doctors, clergymen, lawyers, University Dons, civil servants, business men; it includes two millionaires, three world-famous statesmen, thirty-two knights, eleven peers of the realm, two princes of royal blood and one princess. . . . Why? Why this extraordinary

PERIL AT END HOUSE

AGATHA CHRISTIE
PERIL AT END HOUSE

Poirot returns!

AGATHA CHRISTIE
Author of
THE SITTAFORD MYSTERY

7/6
NET

THE CRIME CLUB

PERIL AT
END HOUSE
by
AGATHA CHRISTIE

THREE near escapes from death in three days! Is it accident or design? And then a fourth mysterious incident happens, leaving no doubt that some sinister hand is striking at Miss Buckley, the charming young owner of the mysterious End House. The fourth attempt, unfortunately for the would-be murderer, is made in the garden of a Cornish Riviera hotel where Hercule Poirot, the famous little Belgian detective, is staying. Poirot immediately investigates the case and relentlessly unravels a murder mystery that must rank as one of the most brilliant that Agatha Christie has yet written.

Read also
THE MURDER OF THE NIGHT CLUB LADY
by ANTHONY ABBOT

MYSTERY IN KENSINGTON GORE
by MARTIN PORLOCK

Left: The front section of a promotional wraparound band. In later years, the bands became slimmer in depth. The design gives a slightly stronger air of menace than usual. Frequently the jackets suggested a lightweight attitude to murder, attractive to readers looking for entertainment.

Peril at End House • 77

PERIL
AT END HOUSE

AGATHA CHRISTIE

Published for
THE CRIME CLUB LTD.
by
W. COLLINS SONS & CO LTD
LONDON

Book Description

The book is a standard demy-octavo volume measuring 190 mm by 125 mm. It consists of 256 pages, and the text begins on page 9 and ends on page 252, followed by a publisher's advertisement section of four pages headed 'New 7/6 Detective Novels'. The book is bound in orange cloth, lettered in black. The striking dust-wrapper shows a figure carrying a lantern against a blue-green background.

Reviews

The critics took to the book, and reviews on both sides of the Atlantic were full of praise. The *Times Literary Supplement* wrote, 'The actual solution is quite unusually ingenious, and well up to the level of Mrs Christie's best stories.' Isaac Anderson in the *New York Times* told his readers, 'This person who is responsible for the dirty work at End House is diabolically clever, but not quite clever enough to fool the little Belgian detective all the time. A good story with a most surprising finish.'

Spin-Offs

On 1 May 1940, the play *Peril at End House* opened at the Vaudeville Theatre in London, after a pre-London tour which had begun on 2 January. Poirot was played by Francis L. Sullivan, who had taken the role in *Black Coffee,* a play Christie wrote featuring Poirot, Hastings and Japp that was first performed in 1930. The character of Jim Lazarus, who had been the subject of some anti-Semitic remarks in the book, was replaced by the non-Jewish Terry Ord, a change necessitated by the fact that England was now at war with Nazi Germany. The play was generally well received. In January 1990, some fifty years later, London Weekend Television first broadcast its adaptation, with David Suchet as Poirot, Hugh Fraser as Hastings and Philip Jackson as Japp.

Opposite above: The Salcombe Hotel today, mostly Edwardian, with this art-deco wing added. This made a very pretty setting, becoming the Majestic Hotel in filming of *Peril at End House,* by Carnival Films. However, the Imperial Hotel, on which Christie's description is based, is far larger.

Opposite below: The title page of the UK edition and the jacket of the first US edition, with perhaps a stronger attempt to create an atmosphere of murder in mind and a rare photograph of the author, known for her shyness, on the rear cover. Only a handful of the UK jackets have Agatha Christie's photograph anywhere to be seen.

THE THIRTEEN PROBLEMS

The Thirteen Problems, London: Collins, The Crime Club, 1932
The Tuesday Club Murders, New York: Dodd, Mead, 1933

Background and Storyline

The book consists of thirteen short stories featuring Miss Marple, of which the first six were originally serialized. In the first story, 'The Tuesday Night Club', Jane Marple is entertaining at home. Her guests include her novelist nephew Raymond West and his fiancée; one Dr Pender, an elderly cleric; Mr Petherick, a local solicitor; Joyce Lempriere, an artist; and Sir Henry Clithering, a retired Commissioner of Scotland Yard. The conversation turns to crime and one of the guests suggests they form a club, to meet each Tuesday, at which a different member will relate a mystery known to themselves to which the others will be encouraged to venture a solution. The first tale is told by Sir Henry and the correct solution is provided by Miss Marple, who continues to out-perform her friends in the succeeding stories. The formula is repeated in a second set of six stories in which Miss Marple's neighbours, Colonel and Mrs Bantry, act as hosts, with a slightly different guest list. The thirteenth story also features Sir Henry, who finds himself involved by Miss Marple in the investigation of a local crime while visiting his friends the Bantrys. The stories are never less than absorbing and are a tribute to Jane Marple's powers of observation: 'human nature is much the same everywhere, and, of course, one has opportunities of observing it at closer quarters in a village'.

Book Description

The volume measures 190 mm by 130 mm and consists of 256 pages of which the text runs from page 9 to 250; the last three leaves advertise 'New 7/6 Detective Novels'. The book is bound in orange cloth lettered in black on the upper cover and spine. The jade-green dust-wrapper is basically typographical with lettering and decoration in black. The inner flaps promote this title and Collins' detective fiction in general and the lower panel promotes The Crime Club. The upper panel features three masked gunmen and the spine a single gunman. They are to become familiar as the logo for The Crime Club.

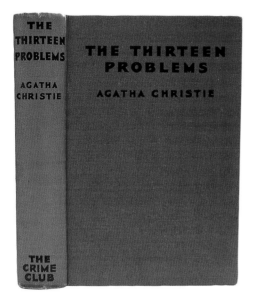

Above: Printed on easily damaged soft paper, the jacket is bold in its use of the colour green. However the design is a little plain and relies on the Crime Club logo and the distinctive Basuto type to market the short stories featuring Miss Marple.

Left: The first UK edition of *The Thirteen Problems*, now very hard to find. Happily, among the jackets sourced for this book, there is not a single one where the owner had cut out the rear section in order to join The Crime Club!

THE HOUND OF DEATH

The Hound of Death and Other Stories, London: Odhams Press, 1933

Background

This collection of twelve stories was published by Odhams Press rather than Collins, probably because Collins was not interested in a collection of stories which had mostly been published already and did not feature Poirot or Miss Marple. It was never published in the USA but all the stories may be found in other anthologies published there. Six are to be found in *Witness for the Prosecution* (1948), five others in *The Golden Ball* (1971) and the remaining story, 'The Last Seance', with seven other stories in *Double Sin* (1961).

Storyline

The stories are difficult to classify but many involve the supernatural and some rely on the powers of extra-sensory perception. The title story tells the legend of a Belgian nun possessed of supernatural powers who is supposed to have blown up her convent when it was occupied by invading German forces during the First World War. All the stories are highly readable but perhaps the best is 'Witness for the Prosecution', which Christie later turned into a play with a different ending. In the story the criminal evaded justice, but twenty years on the author was keen that this should not happen. A film of *Witness for the Prosecution* opened in 1957, with a cast including Charles Laughton, Tyrone Power and Marlene Dietrich.

Book Description

The volume measures 190 mm by 130 mm and consists of 252 pages of which the text occupies pages 7 to 247; the last two leaves are blank. The dramatic upper panel, printed in two shades of green, royal blue, black and white, features a sinister hound against the background of a moonlit graveyard and a ruined church. The author's name is in black at the head and the title is in pale green at the foot. The design wraps onto the spine which is lettered in black, with the green-eyed head of the hound staring out at the reader from mid-spine. The publisher's logo is in white at the foot of the spine.

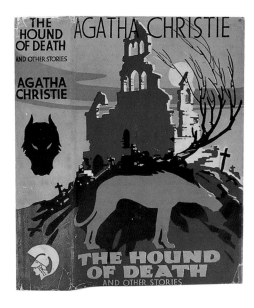

Above left: The Odhams dust-jacket, which is one of the easier designs to obtain today. It is striking and certainly a worthy successor to the Collins designs. The bright blue and green shades were very fashionable in 1933, and widely used across all kinds of products. The flat graphics give a lighthearted but dramatic effect, with the black typeface finishing the jacket off with a contrasting strength.

Above right: The Odhams binding, the book's true first appearance, in a rather dark plain purple, which is fairly easy to find still and is often in good condition.

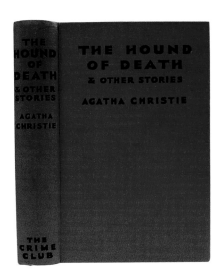

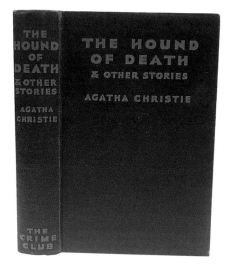

Left: The first cloth-bound editions by Collins, who published the stories after Odhams Press. Two colours were used, the slightly more prolific black cloth, which was also used on reprint bindings with other titles; and the rarer orange cloth.

LORD EDGWARE DIES

Lord Edgware Dies, London: Collins, The Crime Club, 1933
Thirteen at Dinner, New York: Dodd, Mead, 1933

Background and Storyline

This novel – written in Iraq while Christie waas accompanying her husband on an archaeological expedition – is set entirely in the West End of London and features Poirot, Hastings and Japp. At a dinner party the actress Jane Wilkinson admits to Poirot that she needs to be rid of her husband, Lord Edgware; she wishes to remarry but her husband will not give her a divorce. The very next day Japp informs Poirot that Lord Edgware has been murdered. Suspicion naturally falls on his wife and various witnesses insist that they saw Lady Edgware visit her husband shortly before his death. However, she is by no means the only person who wishes to be rid of Edgware, a thoroughly unattractive character. Much play is made of the ability of Carlotta Adams, an American actress and star of a one-woman show, to impersonate a wide range of characters including Jane Wilkinson. The story is beautifully plotted and several surprises are sprung before Poirot, on top form, arrives at the correct solution.

Book Description

The volume measures 190 mm by 130 mm and consists of 256 pages of which the text occupies pages 9 to 252; the last two leaves consist of advertisements. The book is bound in orange cloth lettered in black on the upper cover and spine. The upper panel of the Lambart-designed dust-wrapper, in blue, black and white, shows Lord Edgware slumped over his desk with a knife protruding from his neck. Seated nearby, a tall broad-shouldered man with swept-back grey hair, presumably Inspector Japp, eyes the corpse intently. The spine features Lady Edgware in a blue evening dress, silhouetted against the light. The lettering is in blood red.

Opposite right: The first cloth-bound edition by Collins, still in the format from the 1930–34 period.

Opposite far right: A 1930s veronal box, of the type Carlotta Adams, the second victim, may have used. Veronal was a favourite poison with Agatha, appearing previously in *The Murder of Roger Ackroyd.*

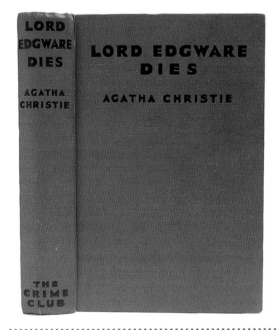

Above: The strong dust-jacket design, with Charles Laughton on the rear cover, in his recent performance as Poirot in *Alibi*, a 1928 adaptation of *The Murder of Roger Ackroyd* at the Prince of Wales Theatre. The rear flap (not shown) has the same design format as for the earlier recent novels, with a section to fill in for new members of The Crime Club.

WHY DIDN'T THEY ASK EVANS?

Why Didn't They Ask Evans?, London: Collins, The Crime Club, 1934
The Boomerang Clue, New York: Dodd, Mead, 1935

Background and Storyline

The book is one of Christie's best, a thriller in which the crime is solved not by a professional but by a couple of rank amateurs: Bobby Jones, the vicar's son, and Lady Frances 'Frankie' Derwent. The title is the final words of the dying man, Alan Carstairs, whom Bobby and his fellow golfer find when looking over the cliffs for a lost ball. The inquest verdict is death by accident but after Bobby mentions the dying man's words in front of the wrong people, an attempt is made on his life and the verdict begins to look distinctly optimistic. The dying man's question is answered but not until very much later and not before Bobby and Frankie have undergone some exciting adventures which include being bound, gagged and left to die in an attic.

Book Description and Spin-Offs

The volume measures 190 mm by 130 mm and consists of 254 pages of which the text occupies pages 7 to 252, the last leaf consisting of advertisements. The book is bound in orange cloth, lettered in black on the upper cover and spine. The upper panel of Gilbert Cousland's dust-wrapper shows the dying Alan Carstairs. The spine shows one of the golfers holding a photograph. In 1980, London Weekend Television filmed the story with a brilliant cast which included James Warwick, Francesca Annis, Sir John Gielgud and Joan Hickson, later to be the definitive Miss Marple.

Opposite above: The UK wrapper is far more enticing and seems to invite one to follow the trail of clues given by the title.

Opposite below left: The first cloth-bound edition by Collins, still in the 1930–34 format. This copy, like many others, has suffered the usual fading to the spine, due to a long time without a jacket.

Opposite below right: The US jacket, with the alternative title *The Boomerang Clue*. The artwork has a sweeping flow but doesn't actually reveal much about the plot.

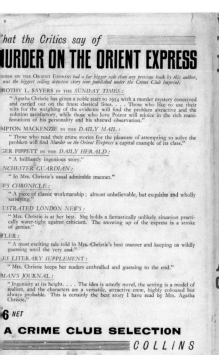

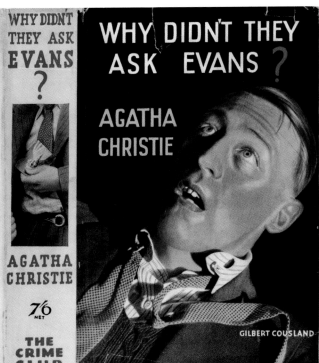

What the Critics say of

MURDER ON THE ORIENT EXPRESS

MURDER ON THE ORIENT EXPRESS had a far bigger sale than any previous book by this author, was the biggest selling detective story ever published under the Crime Club imprint.

DOROTHY L. SAYERS in the SUNDAY TIMES :

"Agatha Christie has given a noble start to 1934 with a murder mystery conceived and carried out on the finest classical lines. . . . Those who like to use their wits for the weighing of the evidence will find the problem attractive and the solution satisfactory, while those who love Poirot will rejoice in the rich manifestations of his personality and his shrewd observation."

COMPTON MACKENZIE in the DAILY MAIL :

"Those who read their crime stories for the pleasure of attempting to solve the problem will find Murder on the Orient Express a capital example of its class."

ROGER PIPPETT in the DAILY HERALD :

"A brilliantly ingenious story."

MANCHESTER GUARDIAN :

"In Mrs. Christie's usual admirable manner."

TP'S CHRONICLE :

"A piece of classic workmanship ; almost unbelievable, but exquisite and wholly satisfying."

ILLUSTRATED LONDON NEWS :

"Mrs. Christie is at her best. She holds a fantastically unlikely situation practically water-tight against criticism. The snowing up of the express is a stroke of genius."

TATLER :

"A most exciting tale told in Mrs. Christie's best manner and keeping us wildly guessing until the very end."

TIMES LITERARY SUPPLEMENT :

"Mrs. Christie keeps her readers enthralled and guessing to the end."

SEAMAN'S JOURNAL :

"Ingenuity at its height. . . . The idea is utterly novel, the setting is a model of realism, and the characters are a versatile, attractive crew, highly coloured but always probable. This is certainly the best story I have read by Mrs. Agatha Christie."

6 NET

A CRIME CLUB SELECTION
COLLINS

WHY DIDN'T THEY ASK EVANS ?

AGATHA CHRISTIE

7/6 NET

THE CRIME CLUB

WHY DIDN'T THEY ASK EVANS ?

AGATHA CHRISTIE

GILBERT COUSLAND

BELIEVE it or not, Bobby Jones had topped his drive ! He was badly bunkered. There were no eager crowds to groan with dismay. That is easily explained—for Bobby was merely the fourth son of the Vicar of Marchbolt, a small golfing resort on the Welsh coast. And Bobby, in spite of his name, was not much of a golfer. Still, that game was destined to be a memorable one. On going to play his ball, Bobby suddenly came upon the body of a man. He bent over him. The man was not yet dead. "Why didn't they ask Evans ?" he said, and then the eyelids dropped, the jaw fell. . . . It was the beginning of a most baffling mystery. That strange question of the dying man is the recurring theme of Agatha Christie's magnificent story. Read it and enjoy it.

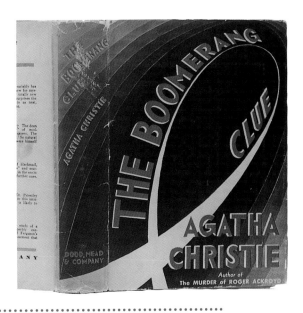

MURDER ON THE ORIENT EXPRESS

Murder on the Orient Express, London: Collins, The Crime Club, 1934
Murder on the Calais Coach, New York: Dodd, Mead, 1934

Background

In 1933, Max Mallowan, with the sponsorship of the British Museum, led an archaeological expedition to Arpachiya, in Iraq, not far from the better-known site at Nineveh where he had dug before. Among the party was his wife, who spent her time writing this novel, one of her most famous. In her autobiography, Christie told how she had seen the coaches for the Orient Express at Calais when boarding trains to other less exotic destinations and had 'longed to climb up into it'. Her wish had been fulfilled several times by the time she wrote the book. Indeed part of her journey to and from Arpachiya was accomplished on the Orient Express, so her command of detail came from recent personal experience.

The book was published in the USA as *Murder in the Calais Coach*, a title which does not have the resonance of the original but which avoided any confusion with Graham Greene's *Stamboul Train* (1932), which had been published in the USA under the title *Orient Express*.

Storyline

Poirot is returning from Syria on the Orient Express following the completion of a mission for the French government, when a murder is committed on the train, which shortly afterwards is halted in the wilds of Yugoslavia by a snow-drift. An old friend of Poirot's who is a director of the railway company is also on the train and appeals for Poirot's assistance in solving the murder – preferably before the train reaches the Italian border. The heavy snowfall makes it impossible for anyone to have left the train and the murderer must therefore still be on board. The passengers, all of whom are suspects, are as colourful a collection of characters as one might expect on such a glamorous express. The murdered man, a shady businessman called Ratchett, has a valet and secretary.

Above: The Orient Express makes a dramatic entrance under the station canopy at Milan in the early 1930s. The company was founded by George Nagelmackers in 1872 as the Compagnie Internationale des Wagons-Lits. The established route to Constantinople was completed in 1889 and a branch to Venice was added by 1907. In 1922 the Calais-Mediterranée Express became the Blue Train (see Agatha Christie's 1928 novel). That year Thomas Cook acquired the Orient Express as agent. In 1930 a route to Aleppo opened the Taurus Express. The service was suspended during the Second World War; it reopened afterwards but 1977 saw the last run of the traditional coaches and routes.

Below: One of the original Orient Express carriages, now operating a luxury service on the Venice Simplon-Orient-Express within Europe.

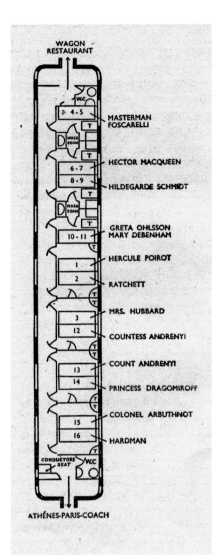

SIMPLON-ORIENT-EXPRESS

TAURUS-EXPRESS

EUROPE
ASIE
AFRIQUE

Above left: The plan of the cabins inside the Orient Express, included in the first edition. Would this help the reader to solve the murder? Only an imaginative person who doesn't already know the answer can tell! Nevertheless, Agatha liked to give her readers a fair chance in every novel, even if some of them disagreed with her sense of fair play.

Above right: A famous poster, advertising the Simplon Orient Express and the Taurus Express, which had been recently launched.

Right: The first cloth binding of the UK edition, still well preserved and the most valuable of the 1930s books for collectors.

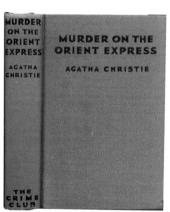

Above: Travel fashions in 1934.

Left: A luxurious wash stand, in use today in a restored 1924 carriage.

There is a Colonel Arbuthnot, a typically stiff-upper-lipped army officer; the Count and Countess Andrenyi, a Hungarian diplomat and his wife; the imperious Russian Princess Dragomiroff and her German maid; a Mrs Hubbard, an irritating American widow; and Swedish missionary Greta Ohlsson. As Poirot continues his investigations, it becomes clear that Ratchett had a distinctly murky past during which he accumulated many enemies.

Employing his little grey cells to good effect, Poirot eventually reaches two possible solutions which he reports to his friend M. Bouc, the director of the railway company, leaving his friend to decide which he prefers. The adoption of either solution would allow the person or persons responsible to go free – making Poirot an accomplice to murder – but this is overshadowed by the nature of the real, as opposed to preferred, solution, which is among Christie's most breathtaking and which gives this book its unique place in the history of the detective story.

THE CREAM OF DETECTIVE FICTION

SELECTED FOR YOU BY THE **CRIME CLUB** PANEL

THE panel of five experts (including Dr. Cyril Alington) selects three detective stories per month and announces them to you, *free of all charge*, in the Quarterly *News*. The books are obtainable, on the First Monday in Every Month, at every bookshop and library.

RETURN COUPON BELOW
YOUR MEMBERSHIP BEGINS AT ONCE

To THE
CRIME CLUB HEADQUARTERS,
48 PALL MALL, LONDON, S.W.1

Please enrol me at once as a member. I understand that no payment or obligation of any kind is attached to membership.

NAME...

ADDRESS..
PLEASE WRITE IN BLOCK LETTERS

....

....

AT EVERY BOOKSHOP AND LIBRARY

Have You Read

LORD EDGWARE DIES

by

Agatha Christie

" It is always a delight to meet Hercule Poirot again. . . . He is one of the few real detectives. . . . *Lord Edgware Dies* is a very good Poirot adventure. Mrs. Christie's touch seems to me to become firmer and her style mellower as she adds book to book. . . . I give it full marks."
DOROTHY SAYERS in the *Sunday Times*.

" We are always glad to have M. Poirot back . . . it is one of Hercule's finest efforts . . . its remarkable ingenuities leave the reader thrilled, but not jaded."
GEORGE SAMPSON in the *Observer*.

" Mrs. Christie is as ingenious, as amiably ironic and amusing as ever . . . the characters are delightful."
E. C. BENTLEY in the *Daily Telegraph*.

" Superlatively good."—*Everyman.*

7/6 *net*

Above: The first edition of the jacket for *Murder on the Orient Express*. This most famous of novels has all the style of the mid 1930s graphic design, using the now standard Basuto typeface. The front cover has a slightly unusual choice of theme, but it still has a dramatic impact today. The earlier novels are all promoted and the contemporary reader is, as always, urged to join The Crime Club.

Opposite: A section at actual size.

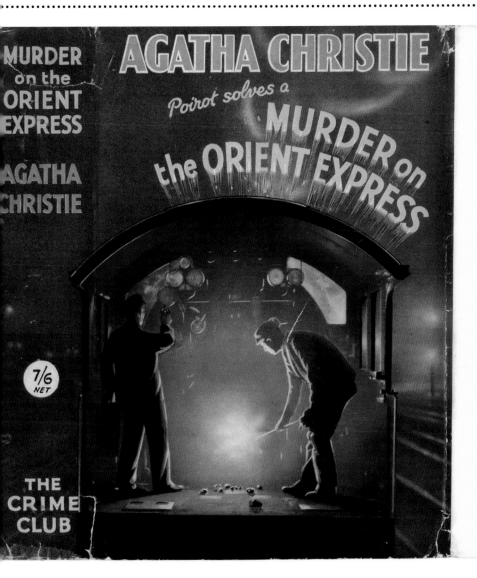

MURDER ON THE ORIENT EXPRESS

by

AGATHA CHRISTIE

THE famous Orient Express, thundering along on its three days' journey across Europe, came to a sudden stop in the night. Snowdrifts blocked the line at a desolate spot somewhere in the Balkans. Everything was deathly quiet. "Decidedly I suffer from the nerves," murmured Hercule Poirot, and fell asleep again. He awoke to find himself very much wanted. For in the night murder had been committed. Mr. Ratchett, an American millionaire, was found lying dead in his berth—stabbed. The untrodden snow around the train proved that the murderer was still on board. Poirot investigates. He lies back and thinks—with his little grey cells. . . . *Murder on the Orient Express* must rank as one of the most ingenious stories ever devised. The solution is brilliant. One can but admire again the amazing resource of Agatha Christie.

Read also
THE ROBTHORNE MYSTERY
by JOHN RHODE

CANDIDATE FOR LILIES
by ROGER EAST

DIRECTORS.
Sir Edmund Wyldbore Smith
Stanley Adams
Lt.-Col. M. R. C. Backhouse, D.S.O.
Baron Giulio Blanc (Italian)
B. D. F. Docker.
Leon J. Gardey (American, formerly Belgian)
Sir Edward Grigg, D.S.O.
R. Margot-Noblemaire (French)
Rt. Hon. Lord Mottistone
Baron R. Snoy (Belgian)
G. Zuccoli (Italian).

HEAD OFFICE :
BERKELEY STREET, LONDON, W.1.
WAREHOUSES :
70-77. COWCROSS STREET, E.C.1.

OFFICES OF THOS. COOK & SON, LTD
AND ASSOCIATED COMPANIES

BARROW-IN-FURNESS   JOHANNESBURG.
BELFAST.   LOS ANGELES.
BIRMINGHAM   MELBOURNE.
BLACKBURN   MOMBASA.
BOLTON.   MONTREAL.
BOURNEMOUTH   NAIROBI.
BRADFORD.   NEW YORK
BRIGHTON   PERTH (W. AUSTRALIA).
BRISTOL.   PHILADELPHIA.
BURNLEY   ST. LOUIS (Mo. U.S.A)
CARDIFF.   SAN FRANCISCO.
CHELTENHAM   SYDNEY.
DUBLIN.   TORONTO.
EASTBOURNE   VANCOUVER.
EDINBURGH.   WASHINGTON
GLASGOW.   (D.C., U.S.A.)

OFFICIAL AGENTS OF
THE PASSION PLAY COMMITTEE,
OBERAMMERGAU, 1934

TELEPHONE NOS. WHITEHALL 1911 TO 1914.
TELEGRAPHIC ADDRESS. "ALLOTMENTS, LONDON."

THOS. COOK & SON, LTD.
WORLD-WIDE TRAVEL SERVICE
ESTABLISHED 1841.
GENERAL FOREIGN PASSENGER AGENTS PENNSYLVANIA RAILROAD

WEST END AGENCY OF UNION-CASTLE LINE TO SOUTH AND EAST AFRICA,
AND FYFFES LINE (ELDERS & FYFFES LTD.) TO WEST INDIES & PANAMA.

PM/POST
17794.

125, PALL MALL,
LONDON. S.W.1.

PLEASE QUOTE THIS REFERENCE

March 26, 1934.

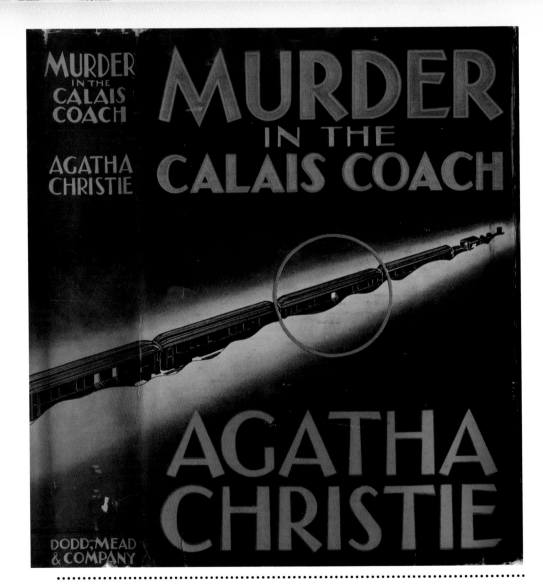

94 • The 1930s

Book Description

The book is a standard demy-octavo volume, measuring 190 mm by 125 mm. It consists of 256 pages, of which the text runs from pages 11 to 254 with two pages of publisher's advertisements. The book is bound in orange cloth, lettered in black. The highly evocative dust-wrapper by an unknown artist shows the driver and fireman hard at work on the footplate as the Orient Express powers through the night. The only illumination is from the fire itself, which allows the artist a certain amount of licence with the detail of the cab, although the cut-out forward-facing window-glasses and cab-side windows are pure LNER.

Opposite top: Thomas Cook's letterhead of 1934. The famous travel company became agents for the Orient Express service.

Reviews

The book was generally enthusiastically received, although Raymond Chandler, the American thriller writer, was fierce in his condemnation of the solution. Compton Mackenzie, writing in the *Daily Mail,* described it as 'a capital example of its class'. Dorothy L. Sayers, perhaps Christie's greatest rival at the time, was generous with her praise. Writing in *The Times*, Sayers called the novel 'a murder mystery conceived and carried out on the finest classical lines'.

Spin-Offs

Agatha Christie had to wait for forty years before the book was turned into a feature film, which turned out to be not only the most profitable British film yet but also a great critical success, receiving six Academy Award nominations. Sidney Lumet directed a stellar cast. Poirot was played by Albert Finney and the murdered man by Richard Widmark, while the other passengers included Sean Connery, Vanessa Redgrave, Wendy Hiller, Lauren Bacall, Ingrid Bergman, Rachel Roberts, Anthony Perkins and Sir John Gielgud. Even Christie, always a severe critic of film versions of her books, acknowledged its excellence, reserving her criticism for the paucity of Finney's moustache.

Opposite: The striking dark-blue front cover and spine of the US jacket, which specifies the coach name and location of the murder. It displays a more stylish design than the British, aided by the powerful colour and strong typeface. Many of the jacket designs in the USA have a more modernist feel than those in the UK at this period. Yet it is the UK designs that have always attracted the collectors, for the very quaintness of the covers and, of course, because Agatha Christie is perceived as the most English of authors, even though she had American roots.

THE LISTERDALE MYSTERY

London: Collins, The Crime Club, 1934

Background and Storyline

The Listerdale Mystery was not published in the USA but all the stories save 'Sing a Song of Sixpence' were anthologised: 'Accident' and 'Philomel Cottage' in 1948 in *Witness for the Prosecution* and the other stories featured in *The Golden Ball* (1971), with the exception of 'Mr Eastwood's Adventure', which had been published in 1965 in *Surprise! Surprise!* The book contains twelve short stories of which seven have a crime element and some a romantic interest. They are all highly readable if occasionally slight. Probably the best known are 'Accident' and 'Philomel Cottage', the former of which, about a murderer who for once remains unapprehended at the end of the story, was reprinted in several collections of crime stories. The latter so entranced actor and playwright, Frank Vosper, that he expanded it into a play, *Love from a Stranger*, which was made into a film in 1937 starring Basil Rathbone and Ann Harding. In 1947 there was an American remake in the UK, called *A Stranger Walked In* to distinguish it from the earlier and better film.

Book Description

The volume measures 190 mm by 130 mm and consists of 256 pages of which the text occupies pages 7 to 250; the last three leaves consist of advertisements. The book is bound in burgundy cloth lettered in silver. The upper panel of the dust-wrapper features the author's name and the title illuminated by the glow of a torch shining upwards from the bottom left corner.

Unfinished Portrait

London: Collins, 1934. This was the second of Christie's novels to appear under the pseudonym of 'Mary Westmacott', adopted in 1930 for *Giant's Bread*. The book, unlike the other five, is autobiographical. Many events in Christie's life are covered in more detail here than in her actual autobiography, and while not particularly good as a novel it is very important for an understanding of the author.

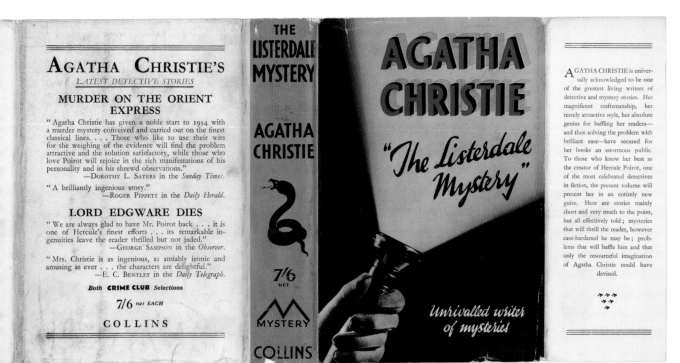

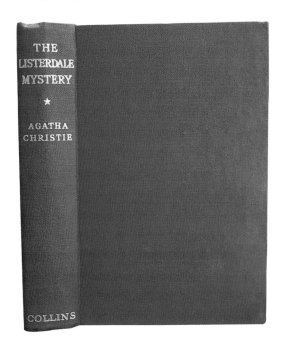

Above: The beautiful jacket of the UK first edition, simple in conception but highly effective. In a slight departure from the standard design, the spine is silver grey and has a snake on it, and the Basuto typeface is not used anywhere on the jacket, except for the Crime Club lettering on the back cover. The casual script on the front is reminiscent of film title sequences.

Right: The burgundy cloth with silver titles.

PARKER PYNE INVESTIGATES

Parker Pyne Investigates, London: Collins, The Crime Club, 1934
Mr Parker Pyne Detective, New York: Dodd, Mead, 1934

Background and Storyline

The book contains twelve short stories. The first six feature cases which Parker Pyne, retired civil servant, has taken on in response to advertisements placed in the personal column of *The Times:* 'Are you happy? If not, consult Mr Parker Pyne, 17 Richmond Street.' Parker Pyne, whose secretary Felicity Lemon is later to assist Hercule Poirot, is possessed of an unshakeable belief that there are only five kinds of unhappiness in the world, and that when the cause has been correctly identified, a solution is guaranteed via his idiosyncratic methods.

The second six stories see Parker Pyne on holiday, where he takes cases when absolutely necessary. He is an inveterate traveller and the stories are all set in the Middle East with which Christie was well acquainted, having accompanied her husband to the area on many archaeological expeditions. Parker Pyne is an interesting and attractive character but critical reaction to the stories went from the dismissive to the 'improves on second reading' variety and Christie only ventured two more stories about him: 'Problem at Pollensa Bay' and 'The Regatta Mystery', both of which were published in the USA in 1939 in a collection named after the latter title and in 1991 in a collection named after the former.

Book Description

The volume measures 190 mm by 130 mm and consists of 256 pages of which the text occupies pages 7 to 248, with three leaves of advertisements. The book is bound in magenta cloth, lettered in silver on the spine. The upper panel of the dust-wrapper features a benevolent Parker Pyne beaming at the reader with, behind him, a less amiable pair of handcuffs.

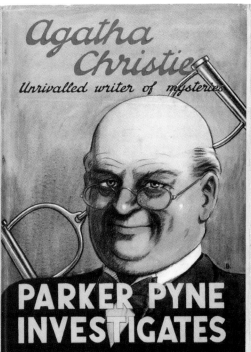

AGATHA CHRISTIE, creator of Hercule Poirot, has now invented an entirely new character, who appears for the first time in the present book. He is Mr. Parker Pyne. Unlike Poirot, he is English, and typically English. Large, not to say fat, with a bald head of noble proportions, he seems to breathe respectability and the pre-eminence of the British Empire. He enjoys a large practice as a private investigator. He is a man of many mysteries and some of these are set down here for the first time. These stories are about the best thing Agatha Christie has done in this particular line, every one a perfect gem of the art of the mystery story.

✤ ✤ ✤

Above: The jacket makes an attempt to define the appearance of Parker Pyne – usually not a good idea, since readers tend to prefer to have their own ideas of the characters. The typeface isn't quite so inventive and elegant as that used for *The Listerdale Mystery.* However the spine is equally successful, with the rear cover and flaps of a similar layout as before.

Right: The magenta purple cloth-bound volume with the silver text as before.

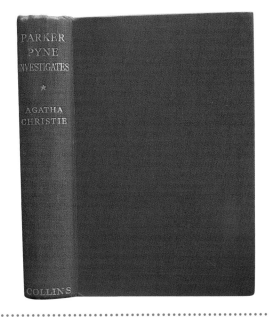

Parker Pyne Investigates • 99

THREE-ACT TRAGEDY

Murder in Three Acts, New York: Dodd, Mead, 1934
Three-Act Tragedy, London: Collins, The Crime Club, 1935

Background, Storyline and Reviews

Well-known actor Sir Charles Cartwright, retired and living in Cornwall, gives a dinner party at which one of his guests dies. Playing important parts in the subsequent drama are Mr Satterthwaite (on one of only two outings outside the Harley Quin stories), the young and attractive Hermione Lytton Gore, Cynthia Dacres, the owner of Ambrosine Ltd, and Hercule Poirot, whose presence is as ever vital. Although not today considered one her best, *Three-Act Tragedy* was well received by the critics and became the first of Christie's books to sell over 10,000 copies in its first year. The reviewer in the *Times Literary Supplement* suggested that 'very few readers will guess the murderer before Mr Hercule Poirot reveals the secret'. Writing in the *New Statesman,* Ralph Partridge summed up the Christie style in words that could be applied to many of her books: 'the power to wrap up clues in the easiest and most natural conversation; the choice of contrasting characters, each outlined with just sufficient sharpness to give them all individuality; the steady pulse of events in chapter after chapter; the originality of the murder plot itself, and the dramatic suspense of the solution hold you until the latest possible minute'.

Book Description

The volume measures 190 mm by 130 mm and consists of 256 pages of which the text runs from pages 13 to 252; the last two leaves consist of advertisements. The book is bound in orange cloth, lettered in black on the upper cover and spine. The upper panel of the dust-wrapper is allusive if uninspired, featuring three full wine glasses. The design wraps over the spine, which repeats the wine-glass motif in miniature. The conceit of the novel as a play is carried on from the title to the list of contents, which list the first five chapters as 'First Act: Suspicion'; the following seven as 'Second Act: Certainty': and the last fifteen as 'Third Act: Discovery'. Likewise, credits feature Sir Charles Cartwright as director, Mr Satterthwaite and Miss Hermione Lytton Gore as assistant directors, clothes by Ambrosine Ltd and illumination by Hercule Poirot.

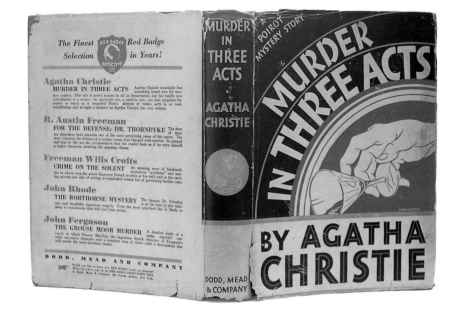

Above: The UK jacket features the poisoned glasses of wine to great effect and the familiar typefaces on the flaps and covers make their appearance once again.

Left: The jacket of the US edition, which was in fact the book's first publication. This one has suffered heavily from damage, yet obviously has been much loved and read.

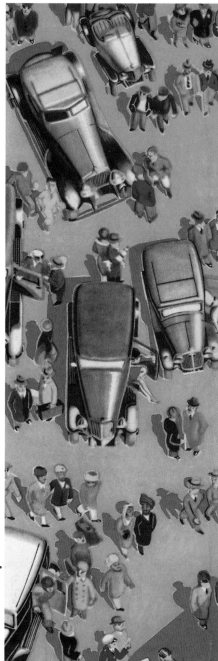

Above: Classic Imperial Airways ephemera, here enticing the customer to try the adventure of travelling abroad, which was of course a luxury for most in the golden age of early flight.

Right: Classic cars depicted in the promotional leaflets illustrate the quaint methods of loading customers' luggage and the process of boarding the flight.

DEATH IN THE CLOUDS

Death in the Air, New York: Dodd, Mead, 1935
Death in the Clouds, London: Collins, The Crime Club, 1935

Background

The second of Christie's crime novels to be published in 1935, *Death in the Clouds* also features Poirot, albeit without his Dr Watson in the form of Arthur Hastings. It is a high-tech variant on the country-house murder story, with an aircraft substituted for the more usual isolated abode.

Dodd, Mead, whose edition preceded the UK edition, changed Christie's intended title (and in so doing duplicated the title of a previously published American short story). Perhaps the American publisher thought their title more evocative of air travel. Whatever the reason, it failed to deflect the author or her UK publishers from staying with her original title.

Storyline

As Poirot is a passenger on the aircraft, he becomes, at least theoretically, a suspect when the discovery is made that one of the ten passengers in the rear compartment of the plane is not sleeping but dead, just a few minutes before the aircraft, on a scheduled flight from Le Bourget, is due to land at London's Croydon Airport. Poirot immediately becomes involved with the investigation in co-operation with his old friend Inspector Japp of Scotland Yard and a M. Fournier of the Sûreté.

Opposite above: A Handley Page 42 passenger aircraft as described in the book, here at Croydon Airport in the early 1930s. The aircraft was first designed for Imperial Airways in 1930–31 for longer flights to the Far East. It featured four engines, and there were two types of layout for slightly varying models. The cabins were divided by crew facilities as can be seen on the internal diagram, overleaf. In all there were eight models, named after mythological figures: Hannibal, Horsa, Hanno and Hadrian, of Eastern-type design, and Heracles, Horatius, Hengist (shown

here) and Helena, of the Western design. In Christie's novel she invents a variant name, the Prometheus. Sadly, by 1941, all had crashed or were irreparably damaged or destroyed. The Heracles operated most flights to Paris at this time, taking two and a quarter hours. None of the models was replaced, but the design contributes a unique presence to detective writing of the 1930s. Freeman Wills Croft also used flying as a central theme in his novel *The 12.30 from Croydon* (1934).

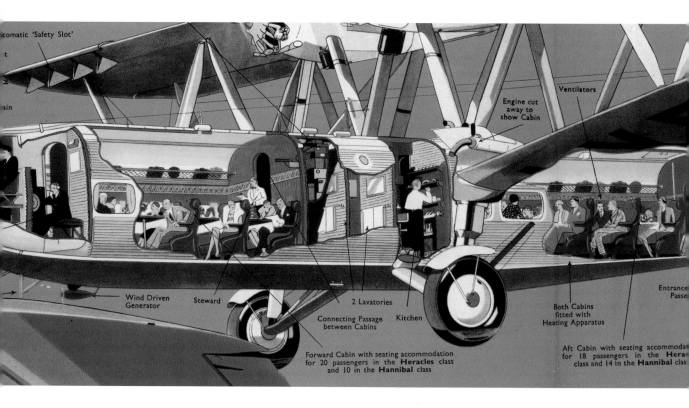

Labels on the illustration: comatic 'Safety Slot'; Ventilators; Engine cut away to show Cabin; Wind Driven Generator; Steward; 2 Lavatories; Connecting Passage between Cabins; Kitchen; Both Cabins fitted with Heating Apparatus; Entrance Passe; Forward Cabin with seating accommodation for 20 passengers in the **Heracles** class and 10 in the **Hannibal** class; Aft Cabin with seating accommoda for 18 passengers in the **Hera** class and 14 in the **Hannibal** clas

Above: The interior of the Handley Page 42, displaying the exact layout of the passenger seating and cabin crew, the scene of the crime in *Death in the Clouds.*

Attention soon focuses on the tiny puncture mark on the throat of the victim, Madame Giselle, which suggests that a poisoned dart or hypodermic has killed her. Whatever the cause, the murder is a bold one, carried out in full view of everyone in the cabin. The passengers include members of the aristocracy, the middle and working classes and, in a private Christie joke at the expense of her archaeologist husband, a couple of men who Japp insists are cut-throats but who turn out to be distinguished archaeologists.

A private note of a different kind interrupts the narrative flow when Christie has the two French archaeologists tell a story about an Englishman who left his sick wife alone in a small hotel in Syria because of the call of work, something which a Frenchman could never have done. The wife was of course Christie herself and evidently the incident rankled. By way of balance, Christie chooses to send up her own profession by including among the suspects an American writer of crime thrillers, who is amusingly identified at one point as Japp's leading suspect. At one point or another, the three detectives suspect each of the passengers and the two stewards in turn. Eventually, of course, it is Poirot, rather than the two professionals, who solves the murder.

Above: The waiting lounge at Croydon Airport, in the mid 1930s.

Left: A timetable listing the prices of the flights. A trip to Paris cost nearly £8, which was very expensive.

IMPERIAL AIRWAYS

Airways House,
Charles Street,
London, S.W.1.

(in conjunction with)
SOCIETE de TRANSPORTS AERIENS RAPIDES (S.T.A.R.)
SERVICE BETWEEN LONDON (via PARIS)
THE HAUTE SAVOIE & THE RIVIERA.
Daily except Sundays.

Read down			SUMMER 1931.		Read up
07.15	dep.	AIRWAYS HOUSE	arr.	19.30
08.00	dep.	CROYDON	arr.	18.45
10.15	arr.	PARIS (Le Bourget)	dep.	16.30
13.15	arr.	DIJON	dep.	14.15
15.15	arr.	GRENOBLE	dep.	12.15
15.50	arr.	CHAMBERY	dep.	11.40
17.00	arr.	CANNES	dep.	10.30
17.15	arr.	34 Gal. Fleuries	dep.	10.15

FARES.	SINGLE.		RETURN.		EXCESS BAGGAGE.	
	Outward	Inward	Outward	Inward	Outward	Inward
London-Paris	£ 4. 4. 0.	F. fcs. 525	£ 7.19.6.	F. fcs 997.50	6d	F fcs. 3.00
„ -Dijon	£ 6. 13. 6.	„ 825	£13.12.6.	„ 1577.50	1/-	„ 6.00
„ -Grenoble	£ 9. 10. 6.	„ 1175	£18. 2. 0.	„ 2235.50	1/7	„ 9.50
„ -Chamber	£10. 2. 0.	„ 1245	£19. 4. 0.	„ 2365.50	1/9	„ 10.20
„ -Cannes	£12. 8. 8.	„ 1525	£23.11. 0.	„ 2897.50	2/2	„ 13.00

Fares include car transport from & to Town centres, 15 kgs (33 lbs) free baggage, allowance per passenger. Intermediate fares on application.

DEATH IN THE CLOUDS

Right: The first UK edition of *Death in the Clouds*, showing Agatha Christie on the back cover. The aeroplane is not the design described in the book. The Basuto typeface is still used by The Crime Club on the base of the spine and inner front flap. However the title-page design was modernised, to a style used for Christie's books for the next fifteen years.

Below: The wraparound band used on promotion. By this date, the bands had become slimmer than in previous years. The fold-in flaps, not shown, were plain white.

Opposite top: The logo of Imperial Airways, the Silver Service.

AGATHA CHRISTIE's
Greatest Poirot Story

DEATH
IN THE
CLOUDS

AGATHA
CHRISTIE

7/6
NET

THE
CRIME
CLUB

DEATH
IN THE
CLOUDS

CRIME CLUB

THE SIGN OF A GOOD
DETECTIVE NOVEL

**DEATH
IN THE
CLOUDS**

by

AGATHA CHRISTIE

OUT of the blue of a September sky the great cross-Channel air-liner *Prometheus* appeared true to time and circled round gracefully to make a perfect landing at Croydon. A plain-clothes inspector accompanied by a uniformed policeman came hurriedly across the aerodrome and climbed into the 'plane. "Will you please follow me, ladies and gentlemen?" The disconcerted passengers were escorted, not into the usual Customs department, but into a small private room, for high over the Channel, death, quick and mysterious, had struck at one of their number. The investigation had begun into what was to prove one of Hercule Poirot's most baffling mysteries. Once again we marvel at the wonderful deductive powers of the little Belgian, perhaps the favourite character in present-day detective fiction.

Read also
**THE MAN
WHO WAS TOO CLEVER**
by A. GILBERT

THE CRIME CLUB
BOOK
OF THE MONTH

Death in the Clouds • 107

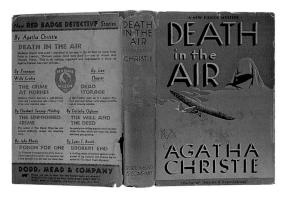

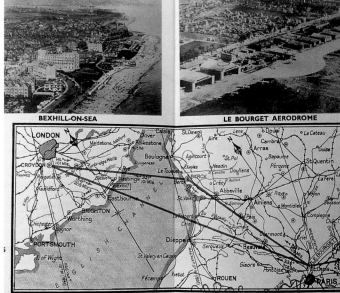

Top left: Darts dipped in curare from Brazil, a poison that Agatha Christie would have come across during her working life at the dispensary. They are longer than those used in the TV drama.

Above left: The US dust-jacket for *Death in the Clouds,* there called *Death in the Air,* which preceded the UK edition. Sadly few copies survive at all well.

Above right: The seating arrangements for the 1935 HP 42 flights were luxurious.

Right: Flight routes to Europe.

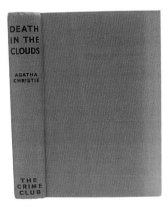

Book Description

The book is standard demy-octavo. The text block measures 183 mm by 124 mm and consists of 256 pages numbered to 252. It is bound in plain orange cloth, lettered on the spine in upper case and printed in black, with the title towards the head, the author's name a little below, and the publisher's imprint, The Crime Club, at the foot. The basic design of the dust-wrapper works well enough, with the design being carried over from the spine onto the upper panel. The spine title and author's name are in blue reversed out of a background of white clouds. The title lettering on the upper panel takes the form of a white vapour trail against the blue background. The aircraft depicted is a little fanciful. The weight and style of lettering is inconsistent and the publisher's assertion that this is Agatha Christie's Greatest Poirot Story would have seemed somewhat exaggerated even at the time.

Left: The UK cloth binding published by The Crime Club.

Reviews

The reviews were a little mixed. The *New York Times* generously described the book as 'a crime puzzle of first quality and mighty entertaining story besides,' while the *Chicago Daily Tribune* was a little more critical, finding the book to be 'entertaining, swift, plausible to a degree, but pretty hard to swallow at the latter end'. The *Times Literary Supplement*'s reviewer probably got it about right with the somewhat delphic assertion 'It will be a very acute reader who does not receive a complete surprise at the end,' which is tantamount to suggesting that there is something of a credibility gap between the plot and the denouement.

Spin-Offs

Death in the Clouds was very successfully filmed as part of the LWT Agatha Christie series starring David Suchet as Poirot and first broadcast in 1992.

THE ABC MURDERS

The ABC Murders, London: Collins, The Crime Club, 1936
The Alphabet Murders, New York: Dodd, Mead, 1936

Above: A typical period railway platform. The plot starts on the southern railway line, on which Hastings arrives at Victoria from the Southampton docks.

Below right: 1936 ladies' fashions by the sea.

Opposite right: The front cover of the 1936 summer Railway Guide. *The ABC Railway Guide* is still in production under a different name, *The OAG Guide.* First published by William Tweedie, *The ABC Guide* made its first appearance in 1853 when train travel was still in its infancy. Advertisements recommended all kinds of benefits for passengers, including revolvers for safety! Oscar Wilde was a noted admirer and Queen Mary insisted on a copy to complete her library in the 1920s. Finally, of course, it made the famous appearance in this, Christie's most famous novel. The *Bradshaw* was its main rival and is referred to in the novel when yet another victim is found dead.

Background

The ABC Murders is one of Christie's best stories and a wonderful contrast to its immediate predecessor, *Death in the Clouds,* in which Poirot's task was simply defined as identifying which of a small group of passengers on a plane had the means and the motive to murder a fellow passenger. In this case, Poirot is challenged to work out the connection between an apparently motiveless series of murders carried out in different parts of the country. It is a challenge which initially perplexes him but to which he rises in due course in magnificent fashion.

Storyline

Hastings, who has left his wife to run their South American ranch and come back to the old country on business, is visiting Poirot in his new flat and finds the great detective puzzled by a letter from someone who signs himself ABC and advises Poirot to look out for Andover on the 21st. Poirot soon discovers that an old woman called Alice Ascher who ran a tobacconist's in Andover was battered to death on the 21st. A second letter from the mysterious ABC recommends Poirot to turn his attention to Bexhill-on-Sea on the 25th of the following month – and Poirot rushes to Bexhill, only to discover that a waitress called Betty Barnard has been found strangled on the beach. As in the first murder, a copy of *The ABC Railway Guide* is found alongside the victim.

The third letter tells Poirot that the scene of the crime is to be Churston in Devon and taunts him with the suggestion that the great detective is past his prime. Poirot and Inspector Japp of Scotland Yard take the sleeper to the West Country only to discover that millionaire Sir Carmichael Clarke has already been killed. Poirot receives a fourth letter informing him that the next murder

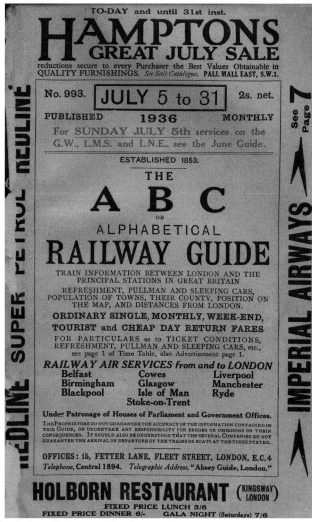

Below: The beach at Bexhill, Sussex, where the B murder takes place.

Right: The splendid interior of Dartmouth station today, which continues to serve passengers who love nostalgia and not least the world of Agatha Christie.

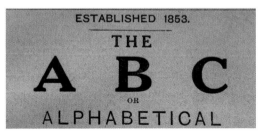

will take place in Doncaster. The murderer strikes a fourth time at a local cinema but something goes wrong; the ABC guide is found by the dead man but the victim's name does not begin with a 'D' but with an 'E', for Earlsfield. A strange dishevelled character called Alexander Bonaparte Cust who was in the cinema seems shocked to discover back at his hotel that he has blood on his cuff and a knife in his pocket. While the police are busy looking for the murderer, Cust staggers into the local police station believing he is guilty of the murders, although he denies having written to Poirot. The police of course assume that Cust is their man but Poirot has other ideas. He has realized all along that the work is not that of a madman who is intent on murdering his way through the alphabet but of someone who is using the alphabet as a cover in order to execute one particular murder for a very specific reason. By the exercise of logic Poirot uncovers the identity of the murderer in a way which is totally convincing and entirely unexpected, leaving the reader satisfied and delighted.

The story was first serialized in the *Daily Express,* which cleverly involved the reader even further by providing an additional column of 'Readers' Guesses', in which one reader had the temerity to take Christie to task for not getting her detective to the projected murder scene quickly enough through failure to read *The ABC Railway Guide* sufficiently carefully.

Top left: A period poster for train travel with the Great Western Railway in Churston station, the village where the third victim, Sir Carmichael Clarke, is found.

Top right: Churston station is still in use on the Dartmouth to Paignton railway line, which runs a steam-powered service.

Opposite left: The De La Warr Pavilion at Bexhill-on-Sea made a stylish café for victim Betty Barnard's workplace in the television drama. The café in the novel was not nearly as glamorous.

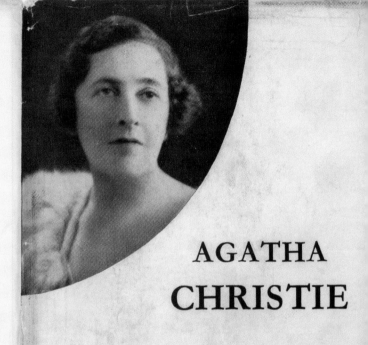

More Poirot
Stories by
Agatha Christie
▼

DEATH IN THE
CLOUDS

"Agatha Christie has succeeded even more triumphantly than usual."
TORQUEMADA in the *Observer*

7/6 net

THREE ACT
TRAGEDY

"Brilliant . . . this is detective writing at its best. Poirot, too, is here. Need one say more?"
SETON DEARDEN in *Time and Tide*

3/6 net

MURDER ON THE
ORIENT EXPRESS

"A piece of classic workmanship . . . exquisite and wholly satisfying."
News Chronicle

3/6 net

AGATHA
CHRISTIE

"*The best of all crime novelists.*"
BYSTANDER

"*Her gift is pure genius.*"
TORQUEMADA

"*What can one do but praise her?*"
SKETCH

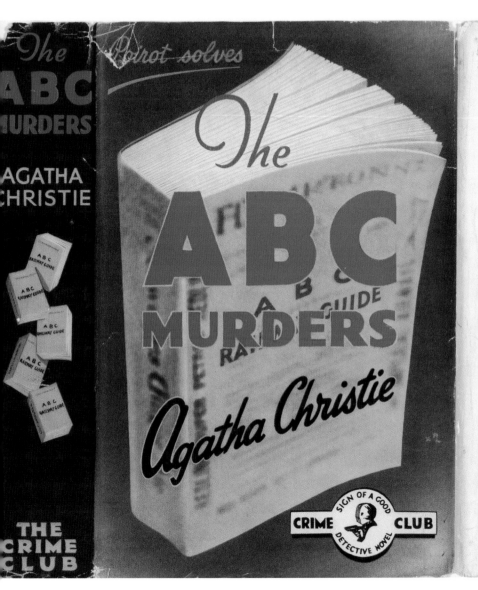

Poirot solves

The ABC MURDERS

AGATHA CHRISTIE

The
ABC
MURDERS

Agatha Christie

CRIME CLUB
SIGN OF A GOOD DETECTIVE NOVEL

THE CRIME CLUB

AGATHA CHRISTIE, "the best of all crime novelists," has, as one critic truly says, "set herself such a standard that even she will scarcely excel it." Yet year by year, book by book, her ingenuity increases, her power as a novelist develops, and her wit becomes keener. Now, with The A B C Murders, her own greatest triumph and a classic of crime fiction, she sets a new high-water mark in the history of the detective story.

The idea of the story is as brilliant as its execution. The murderer in this case is evidently a maniac, for he seems bent on working his way through a whole alphabet of victims. Beginning with A, he murders a Mrs. Ascher at Andover. Proceeding to B, he strangles Betty Barnard on the beach at Bexhill. For C, he chooses as his victim Sir Carmichael Clarke of Churston. And as a sign of his method he leaves beside the corpse on each occasion a railway A B C open at the name of the place where the murder has taken place. A B C . . . how far through the alphabet will he get. It seemed that nobody would be able to catch him. But he made the mistake—the one mistake that every murderer makes—when, out of sheer vanity, he challenged Poirot to frustrate his plans.

In recommending this story to your friends, please do not hint at anything that might spoil their pleasure in reading it.

7/6 Net

Above: The first edition of *The ABC Murders,* openly showing the railway guide connection on the front cover. No doubt it attracted more buyers in search of adventure! The spine is a dark brown-black and the red typeface at the top of the spine is often faded to yellow. Here we see an elegant rather wistful Agatha on the rear cover, as for *Death in the Clouds.* The last copy in this condition sold for over £8000 in 2001. Most jackets of Agatha Christie novels from 1934 to 1939 in fine condition would sell for at least this today; the demand and prices are rising each year at a speed unparalled by the works of any other crime writer.

Opposite: A detail at full size.

Poor Mr Poirot, -

Not so good at these little criminal matters as you thought yourself, are you? Rather past your prime perhaps? Let us see if you can do any better this time. This time it's an easy one. Churston on the 30th. Do try and do something about it! It's a bit dull having it all my own way, you know!

Good hunting, Ever yours
                    A.B.C

Book Description

The book is a standard demy-octavo volume measuring 190 mm by 125 mm. It is bound in orange cloth, lettered in black and consists of 256 pages of which the text runs from pages 9 to 252 with four leaves of publisher's advertisements. The striking dust-wrapper by an unknown artist features the yellow ABC guide beneath red title lettering on the upper panel. The author's name is printed in black. The top left-hand corner features the words 'Poirot solves' and the bottom right-hand corner bears the now familiar Crime Club logo printed in black on white. The spine displays five copies of the ABC guide, one more than the number of murders.

Reviews

The reviewer for *The Times* declared: 'Mrs Christie has invented an entirely new plot for a detective story … she is to be congratulated.' Francis Iles in the *Daily Telegraph* agreed: 'An entirely original idea.' The *Morning Post* trumpeted, 'An Agatha Christie triumph.'

Spin-Offs

Thirty years after the book first appeared, MGM made a film version at Elstree with the title *The Alphabet Murders*. Frank Tashlin, an American director with a background in comedy, was brought in to direct the film which was played for laughs by a cast which included Tony Randall as Poirot and Robert Morley as Hastings. The script, the work of David Pursall and Jack Seddon, made a mockery of the book, and Christie, unsurprisingly, hated every second of it. The 1992 television film, first shown on London Weekend Television with David Suchet as Poirot, Hugh Fraser as Hastings and Philip Jackson as Japp, was a minor triumph. It restored the original title, adhered strictly to period settings and stuck faithfully to the substance and spirit of the original work.

Opposite centre: The challenge Poirot receives from the murderer would entice any reader to attempt to solve the riddle.

Opposite bottom left: The US jacket was totally different from the UK version, and tries to picture the murderer on the front cover, which might be seen as giving too much away. As ever Christie uses her ingenuity to great effect, coming up with an amazing yet fair solution.

Opposite above and below right: Modernist housing near Churston, Devon. Sir Carmichael Clarke's large home came from this period. It is described as modest but for a large gallery housing his collection of artifacts.

Opposite top left: The first UK cloth edition, now just the spine is lettered in black.

MURDER IN MESOPOTAMIA

London: Collins, The Crime Club, 1936
New York: Dodd, Mead, 1936

Background

Above: Desert travel in 1936.

1936 found Max Mallowan, accompanied by his wife, working on the archaeological dig at Chagar Bazar in Syria along with other volunteers and locally recruited labour. The spring season was wet and all the more tolerable for it, but the autumn dig, after the fierce heat of the summer sun had abated, produced major finds that justified Mallowan's decision to dig in that location: seventy cuneiform tablets that demonstrated a connection between the site and the Assyrian royal family around the year 1800 BC.

Christie, as usual, continued to devote what little spare time she enjoyed to the writing of her detective stories. Far from turning her back on her immediate surroundings and writing stories full of nostalgia for a far-off England, she used the material to hand. This novel, dedicated 'to my many archaeological friends in Iraq and Syria', is set in that area of Iraq between the Tigris and Euphrates rivers which used to be called Mesopotamia and features murder on an archaeological expedition. Poirot again features as the visitor with the necessary skills to solve the murder mystery, probably because Christie did not want to invent a new detective and thought that Poirot with his myriad connections and language skills would look distinctly less out of place than Jane Marple.

Below: Flights to the Middle East with Imperial Airways.

CAIRO - BAGHDAD - KARACHI - AIR SERVICE

IMPERIAL AIRWAYS LTD

Above: Transport in the Middle East, 1926, ten years before the novel was published. Desert transport needed to last some years and motorcars had to be equipped for the fierce conditions.

Right: Gertrude Bell on an archaeological dig in 1926, illustrating the rather British attire worn by the teams in those days.

Murder in Mesopotamia • 119

Above: A large courtyard in Baghdad, of similar design to the murder scene in *Murder in Mesopotamia*. The puzzle or riddle model, with a closed situation and a seemingly impossible crime committed, was a favourite for Christie.

Storyline

For once, it is not Hastings who acts as amanuensis for Poirot. We must assume that the former is far too busy with his new wife on their ranch in Argentina to be involved and the job is given to Amy Leatheran, a nurse, who is taken on by the American expedition leader, Dr Leidner, to look after his wife Louise, who has been suffering from terrifying hallucinations.

Murder in Mesopotamia is to some extent a roman à clef and it is the only novel which, according to Mallowan in his autobiography, gave his wife any worries about the possibility of a libel case. Fortunately, the distinguished archaeologists on whom the Leidners were based never cottoned on; or if they did, decided to let the matter pass, perhaps reckoning that very few of Christie's readers would make the connection. Amy Leatheran has elements of Christie herself; the leader of the expedition, Dr Eric Leidner, has features in common with Leonard Woolley with whom Mallowan and Christie had worked; the character of Louise Leidner is again only too obviously based on Katharine Woolley, whose overbearing personality made life difficult and occasionally unbearable for well-nigh everyone who came into contact with her. Her own husband did not escape Christie's attention and recognized himself as the basis for the character of David Emmott, the assistant archaeologist.

Louise Leidner is quickly flagged as the victim; she is clearly terrified by a man she claims has stalked her across the globe. That nobody on the dig believes her heightens her anguish, until she is discovered bludgeoned to death. Poirot soon discovers that practically everyone within a considerable radius of the dig had a substantial motive for wishing her dead. Like Katharine Woolley, Louise Leidner is on her second marriage, but threatening letters apparently from her dead first husband have been arriving at intervals for some time. Poirot's deliberations are briefly stalled by the murder of a second woman, this time by poison, but he eventually unravels the crimes with his customary elan – although the solution might be beyond the thought processes of some readers.

Above left: 1936 fashions for young ladies.

Above: Imperial Airways' colourful brochure of the tourist route across the Middle East.

Left: An aerial view taken of the dig in Mesopotamia, taken by Max and Agatha Mallowan.

MURDER IN MESOPOTAMIA

Agatha Christie

"The only consistently inspired practitioner of an art where ingenuity and industry have so often to substitute for genius."
TORQUEMADA
in the OBSERVER

"The most subtle and ingenious writer of crime fiction alive to-day."
NEWS CHRONICLE

"What can one do but praise her." SKETCH

"What on earth should we do without her."
V. SACKVILLE WEST

MORE "POIROT" STORIES

THE ABC MURDERS
"Once more our homage is due to Mrs. Christie, who has held the throne of detection for the last ten years, and brooks no rival near her."
NEW STATESMAN

DEATH IN THE CLOUDS
"Once more Poirot steps into the limelight of success. . . . Agatha Christie and Poirot, the best combination in modern detective literature.
TIME and TIDE

THREE-ACT TRAGEDY
"Once more Agatha Christie, the best of all crime novelists, introduces to readers that prince of detectives, Hercule Poirot." BYSTANDER

Above: The first-edition jacket of *Murder in Mesopotamia,* by Robin Macartney, a regular colleague on the digs who designed four dust-wrappers in total for Christie. Here he depicts a stylised scene of a dig in historic times. The pale cream background always makes this jacket hard to obtain in a clean condition. This jacket varies in different printings between a cooler colour scheme of blue shades, and here where green dominates more. Other surviving copies sometimes become much paler and look rather washed out. Earlier novels by Christie are promoted on the back cover.

Opposite: A section at full size.

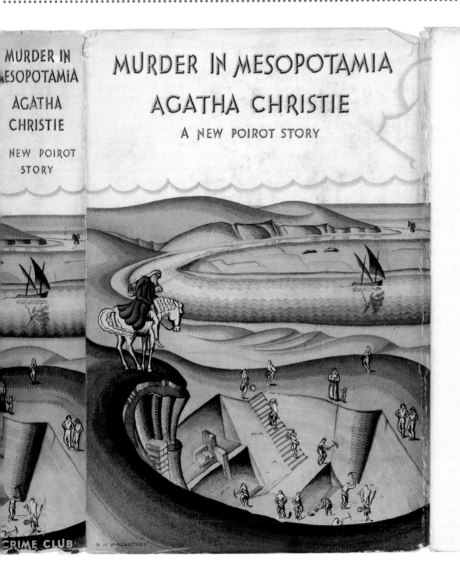

MURDER IN MESOPOTAMIA
AGATHA CHRISTIE
A NEW POIROT STORY

AGATHA CHRISTIE and Hercule Poirot—" the best combination in modern detective literature " —bring all their wit and wits to bear on the solution of another remarkable case.

This time the murder takes place among the members of an expedition which has gone to Mesopotamia to excavate the ruins of an ancient city. As to the murderer, he was so diabolically clever that he would certainly have gone undetected if Poirot had not providentially been passing through on his way to Bagdad. And never, perhaps, has that keen brain been put to a greater test. The story is told by a hospital nurse attached to the expedition, and to have kept the whole tale in character as it would appear to her commonsense mind and professional eye is not the least of Mrs. Christie's achievements.

The unusual setting is not only vividly but authentically described, for Agatha Christie is the wife of an eminent archaeologist and she actually wrote this story while accompanying him in one of his expeditions to Mesopotamia.

7/6 Net

Murder in Mesopotamia • 123

Book Description

The book is a standard demy-octavo volume, measuring 196 mm by 126 mm. It is bound in the usual orange cloth, lettered in black on the spine, and the text runs from pages 9 to 284 plus four pages of advertisements. The striking dust-wrapper, like that of *Death on the Nile,* was designed by Robin Macartney, the architect and painter who accompanied the Mallowans on several archaeological expeditions to the Middle East.

Reviews

'We very much doubt if she has ever given us a better story,' averred the *Evening News*, an opinion shared by the *Daily Mail*: 'As good as anything Mrs Christie has yet given us, and by that I intend very high praise.'

Spin-Offs

For obvious reasons this book was not considered adaptable for the stage. Its setting was also probably seen as too close to that of *Death on the Nile* for it to be considered suitable for a big feature film. It was not until the year 2000 that London Weekend Television chose to adapt it for TV with David Suchet as the definitive Poirot; an adaptation which was, as usual, highly acclaimed, and notable for its very beautiful costumes and scenery.

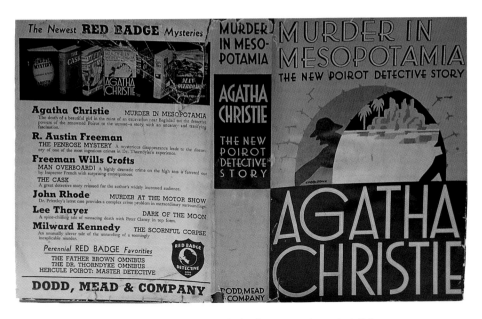

Above: The US jacket has a lively design with the latest typefaces in full flow.

Below: A section of the UK first edition bound in orange cloth; the title is absent from the front board; the title pages.

Opposite: Agatha Christie on excavation at the Chagar Bazar in 1936. Many of the photographs that the Mallowans took are still beautifully preserved in public and private collections as glass and celluloid monochrome negatives, revealing a clear picture of life in the desert. Quite a number of her novels were written on her portable typewriter in a tent, whilst Mallowan and his team were on excavation nearby. One in particular, *Lord Edgware Dies*, had an entirely different setting to the one the author was experiencing.

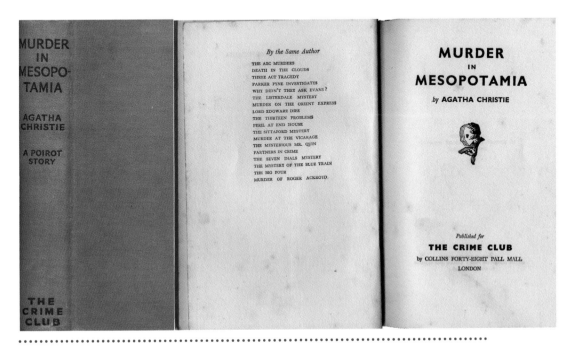

CARDS ON THE TABLE

London: Collins, The Crime Club ,1936; New York: Dodd, Mead, 1937

. . . .

Storyline

Opposite above: The rather restrained UK jacket. Here the green is a perfect mid 1930s shade used in many areas of design at this time.

This is one of Christie's most brilliant crime novels and one in which she warns her readers in her foreword that they are in for something different from the usual detective story. The action takes place in the Park Lane flat of a Mr Shaitana who invites four criminal investigators and four allegedly successful murderers to an evening of bridge. When Poirot, Battle, Race and Ariadne Oliver have finished their five rubbers, they go into the other room where their host has been sitting and find the rubber still in progress and their host sitting by the fire with a dagger in his chest. One of those present has murdered Shaitana, but which one? Was it the young woman who may have poisoned her employer? The doctor who may have hastened the death of annoying patients? The major who may have killed a botanist on an expedition? Or the widow whose husband died in suspicious circumstances? The ending is clever and unexpected, and Poirot considered it one of his favourite cases.

Continued from front flap

another. As Mrs. Christie writes in her preface, "They are four widely divergent types, the motive that drives each one of them is peculiar to that person, and each one would employ a different method. The deduction must, therefore, be entirely *psychological* and when all is said and done, it is the *mind* of the murderer that is of supreme interest."

No wonder Poirot called it one of his most interesting cases. All Mrs. Christie's readers will emphatically agree.

Book Description

Opposite right: The US wrapper has a very lively design in contrast to the slightly plain yet elegant UK edition.

Opposite far right: The UK cloth binding.

The volume measures 197 mm by 130 mm and consists of 288 pages of which the text occupies pages 9 to 286. The last leaf is blank. The book is bound in orange cloth, lettered in black on the spine. The dust-wrapper is a pedestrian affair with a dark-green upper panel and spine, each decorated with playing cards. The Crime Club logo is present at the foot of the upper panel and, in addition to the author's name and the title, the words 'A Poirot Story' in calligraphic lettering appear on the upper panel and spine.

. . . .

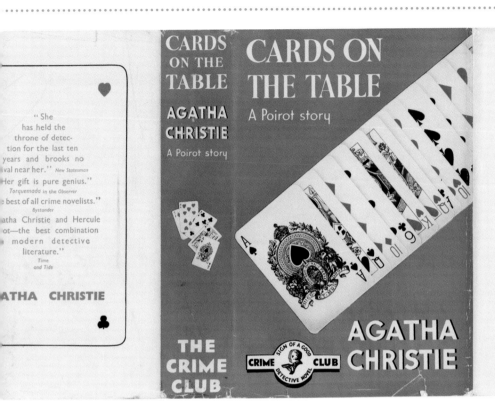

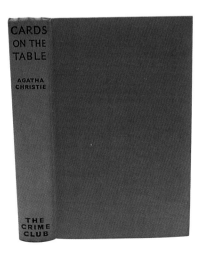

DUMB WITNESS

Dumb Witness, London: Collins, The Crime Club, 1937
Poirot Loses a Client, New York: Dodd, Mead, 1937

Storyline

The story is set in a small country town called Market Basing. It begins with a long rambling letter to Hercule Poirot from an elderly spinster called Emily Arundell who requests his assistance but does not properly explain why. For reasons which are never explained the letter takes two months to arrive. Poirot and Hastings call on Miss Arundell, only to discover that she died of a heart attack several weeks ago. Poirot decides the death is suspicious and proceeds to investigate.

Although not one of Christie's best, the story has many elements which should provide comfort for the aficionado. Set in a small country town, it's a domestic murder with a small number of suspects and involves death by poison. The book commends itself particularly to dog lovers. Some readers may find the developing relationship between Hastings and Bob the wire-haired terrier somewhat hard to take – it includes dialogue and ends with Hastings taking Bob back to his wife and ranch in Argentina – but the dog does play a plausible part in the plot and is an engaging character. Hastings, incidentally, was not to reappear in the Christie canon until *Curtain,* Poirot's final case, in 1975. In 1997, LWT televised the story with David Suchet as Poirot.

Later reprints change the title to *Mystery at Littlegreen House* or *Murder at Littlegreen House.*

Book Description

The volume measures 195 mm by 130 mm and consists of 320 pages of which the text runs from pages 9 to 316; the last two leaves consist of advertisements. The book is bound in orange cloth, lettered in black on the spine. The brown upper panel and spine of the dust-wrapper feature the author's wire-haired fox terrier Peter, to whom the book is dedicated: 'To Dear Peter, most faithful of friends and dearest of companions. A dog in a thousand.'

If it hadn't been for me, old Monsieur Poirot would never have solved this case. Bob

- the *not* so dumb witness!

Agatha Christie's own dog, Peter, to whom this book is dedicated, posed for the photograph on the jacket, but disclaims any connection with the events of the tale. The photograph is reproduced by courtesy of Malcolm Nicholson.

7/6 NET

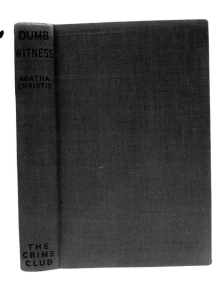

Above: The dust-jacket, featuring the loveable fox terrier who is the star of the novel. The flaps and promotion in general are unusually minimal. The rear flap, not shown is blank.

Left: The UK title page and cloth-bound edition.

DEATH ON THE NILE

London: Collins, The Crime Club, 1937
New York: Dodd, Mead, 1937

Background

In early 1937 Max Mallowan found himself back in the Middle East again, this time leading an archaeological expedition to Tell Brak in Syria, a site which was to prove to be of great importance. Once again, he was accompanied by his wife, who used such free time as she had to write another crime thriller set against a Middle Eastern background, but this time in Egypt, which she and her husband had visited on holiday, rather than Syria or Iraq where her husband had dug. Christie also wrote in the same year a play set in ancient Egypt, *Akhnaton*, but this was destined not to see the light of day for over thirty years. Writing in her autobiography many years later, Christie referred to *Death on the Nile* fondly, considering it to be one of the best of her 'foreign travel' books and with principal characters who seemed to her 'to be real and alive'. Her opinion was certainly endorsed by the critics at the time of publication and then and later by her many fans, who revelled in the exotic setting, the vibrancy of the characterization and the intricacy of the plot.

Above: An atmospheric depiction of feluccas on the Nile, by the Victorian artist David Roberts.

Below: The Mallowans' record of the Nile, looking across to Luxor.

Opposite: A Victorian map of the Nile; the style the feluccas are drawn in inspired the jacket design of the novel.

Storyline

Christie uses the opening chapter to acquaint the reader with the principal characters and to set out their various reasons for wanting to travel to Egypt and take a Nile cruise on the steamer *SS Karnak* from the First to the Second Cataract, with a break at the Cataract Hotel at Aswan. We meet the young, attractive and very wealthy Linnet Ridgeway, who steals Simon Doyle, boyfriend of her oldest friend Jacqueline de Bellefort, now penniless following the stock-market crash, and marries him, to the fury of her former friend, who resolves to haunt the newlyweds by turning up at their honeymoon in Egypt. Linnet and Simon think they have eluded the vengeful Jacqueline and are horrified to discover she is among the small group of passengers on the river steamer. The group, a classic Christie collection, includes Poirot, who is on holiday (and giving every appearance of barely tolerating it), and one Colonel Race, whom Poirot knows slightly and who is working for what we would now call MI6. There is,

Above: An evocative view of Cairo in the Victorian era, again by David Roberts

almost inevitably, a wealthy elderly American woman, Washington socialite Mrs Van Schuyler, travelling with her companion, and a third American in the person of Linnet Ridgeway's lawyer, whose appearance in the group is, he insists, entirely fortuitous. Other characters include an eccentric lady novelist with daughter in tow, an idiosyncratic Italian archaeologist, a suitably abrasive young man of socialist leanings and yet another lawyer, this time an English solicitor.

Colonel Race lets on that he suspects that a well-known agitator and murderer is travelling on the boat, but when the first murder comes, it is not an obviously political target but the unlikeable Linnet. Poirot and Race take charge of the investigation and there are two further murders before Poirot solves the intricate case, in which the brooding and mysterious presence of the Egypt of the Pharaohs exerts a powerful pull.

Opposite clockwise from top: The steamer on the Nile, taken by the Mallowans outside the Winter Palace Hotel in the 1930s; hot weather fashions of 1937; a felucca on the Nile, taken by the Mallowans.

DEATH ON THE NILE

DEATH OF THE NILE

AGATHA CHRISTI

Recent Poirot novels
by Agatha Christie

DUMB WITNESS

" She adds a terrier so fascinating that even Poirot himself is nearly driven from the centre of the stage.''   Manchester Guardian

CARDS ON THE TABLE

'' Agatha Christie at her best. And what more could any one want ? The characters are brilliantly drawn.''   Sunday Times

MURDER IN MESOPOTAMIA

'' As neat a story of crime and detection as you are likely to come across East or West of Suez.''
      Bystander

AGATHA CHRISTIE

" The best of all crime novelists.''   Bystander

" She has held the throne of detection for the last ten years, and brooks no rival near her.''
      New Statesman

" The most subtle and ingenious writer of crime fiction alive to-day.''   News Chronicle

" What on earth should we do without her.''
      V. Sackville West

" Agatha Christie and Hercule Poirot, the best combination in modern detective literature.''   Time and Tide

" She has written over twenty full-length detective tales, and each one is a ' corker.' ''
      St. John Ervine

" Her gift is pure genius . . . that fairy gift of leading readers around by the nose.''
      Torquemada

" Before her fertility of invention the average detection-writer can only bite the dust.''
      Nicholas Blake

" She gives the highly enjoyable impression that both she and the reader are taking part in a mutually exciting game.''   London Mercury

" A model to writers of detective tales.''
      E. R. Punshon

DEATH OF THE NIL

AGATHA CHRISTI

THE CRIME CLUB

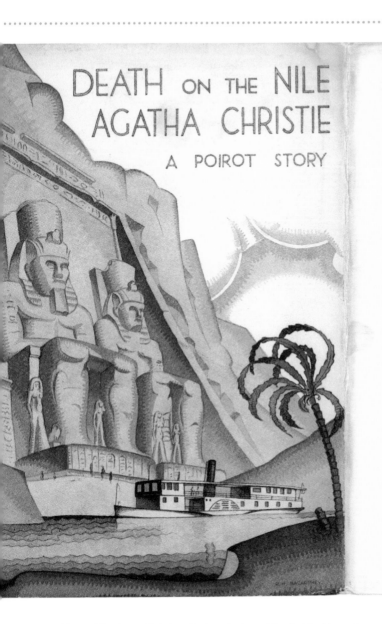

DEATH ON THE NILE
AGATHA CHRISTIE
A POIROT STORY

MRS. CHRISTIE in her new long novel takes us for a journey down the Nile and adds one more to the mysteries of Egypt. She has never collected together a more variegated and interesting group of characters than for this journey during which murder is committed, and with her own knowledge of the Near East she creates the atmosphere so perfectly that one cannot believe, on finishing the book, that one has not made that very self-same journey.

Coming events cast their shadows before them. We feel the death on the Nile long before it occurs. The victim, a girl who has everything—beauty, wealth, love—moves onward to death. We see danger slowly converging upon her from different quarters of the world. Hercule Poirot has been a spectator of the drama from an early moment. He foresees the inevitable end, but is powerless—his advice is disregarded. The murderer is among a little group of people isolated on a steamer far from civilisation. The facts seem to point overwhelmingly to one person—but Poirot is doubtful. He studies the psychology of the crime—bold, audacious and brilliant—and is thereby led to the surprising truth.

7s. 6d.
net

Above: The beautiful dust-jacket designed by Robin Macartney, a colleague on the digs with the Mallowans, who created four jackets for Agatha's books. This is one of his most beautiful and perhaps one of the most stunning in all jacket design history. The style of drawing certainly harks back to the Victorian map-makers, particularly the artwork on the spine. This jacket often survives well, if it survives at all.

Opposite: An actual-size detail featuring the famous temple at Abu Simbel.

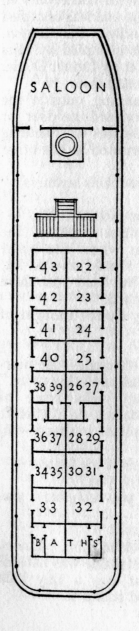

S.S. KARNAK

PROMENADE DECK

SALOON

43	22 JAMES FANTHORP
42	23 TIM ALLERTON
41 CORNELIA ROBSON.	24 MRS ALLERTON
40 JACQUELINE DE BELLEFORT	25 SIMON DOYLE
38 39 ANDREW PENNINGTON	26 27 LINNET DOYLE
36 37 DR BESSNER	28 29 MISS VAN SCHUYLER
34 35 MRS AND MISS OTTERBOURNE	30 31 HERCULE POIROT
33 MISS BOWERS	32 COLONEL RACE

PLAN   CABINS

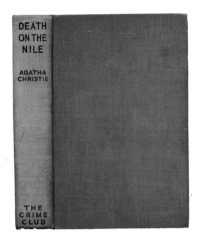
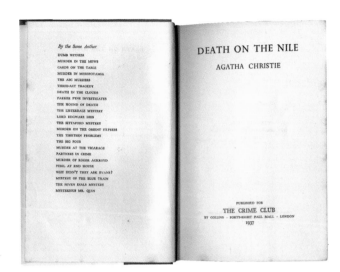

Book Description

The book is a standard demy-octavo volume, measuring 196 mm by 126 mm, bound in orange cloth and lettered in black on the spine. The text runs from pages 9 to 284 with four pages of advertisements. The dust-wrapper is one of several by the architect and painter Robin Macartney, who accompanied Christie and her husband on several expeditions. It shows the *SS Karnak* close to the huge brooding presence of two of the four colossal figures of Ramses, guarding the entrance to the great temple cut out of the rockface at Abu Simbel.

Above left: The UK first edition bound in orange cloth, rather plain compared to the reputation of the novel inside.

Above right: The title pages.

Reviews

The book went down extremely well with the critics, some of whom were extravagant with their praise. Milward Kennedy, writing in the *Sunday Times,* described *Death on the Nile* as 'a peach of a case for Poirot. I take off my hat to the author for as ingenious an alibi as can well be imagined'. In *The Observer,* Torquemada commented, 'The main alibi is of the first brilliance … the descriptive work hits, as it were, the Nile on the head.' The *Evening News* was also enthusiastic: 'She has excelled herself … must call for unqualified praise.' The reviewer for *The Times* was less gushing but as admiring when he wrote, 'Must be read twice, once for enjoyment and once to see how the wheels go round.'

Spin-Offs

In 1945 Christie adapted *Death on the Nile* for the stage, changing the title to *Murder on the Nile*. The plot remained substantially the same although the ending was changed. The main difference was that Christie chose to remove Poirot from the proceedings – not for the first or the last time. Her autobiography gives no reason for sacking her great detective. One can only conclude that she felt either that Poirot as a character did not work on stage or that, of the actors available, there was none who commended himself for the part. The character of Poirot was replaced by Father Borrondale, perhaps prompted by a respectful backward glance at Chesterton's Father Brown. There were fewer characters in the stage version and a number of name changes were made for reasons which have never been explained. The play opened at the Wimbledon Theatre in 1945 for its pre-West End run before moving to the Ambassadors Theatre in March 1946. There was a New York opening in September under the feeble title of *Hidden Horizon*, but this was not a success, closing after only a fortnight.

In 1977, after the huge success of *Murder on the Orient Express*, John Brabourne and Richard Goodwin announced plans to film *Death on the Nile*. They had hoped to recruit Albert Finney as Poirot following his brilliant performance in the earlier film but were unable to agree the terms he wanted. Instead, Peter Ustinov got the part. It was a good choice. Ustinov turned in an intelligent and thoughtful performance which was complemented by a stellar cast which included David Niven as Colonel Rice, Bette Davis as the Washington socialite and Maggie Smith as her long-suffering maid. The excellent screenplay was by Anthony Shaffer and the director was John Guillerman. *Variety* magazine, reviewing the film in its issue of 18 September 1978, commented, '*Death on the Nile* is a clever, witty, well-plotted, beautifully produced and splendidly acted screen version of Agatha Christie's mystery.'

Opposite above: A view across the Nile from the Winter Palace Hotel, taken by the Mallowans.

Opposite below: Sailing on a felucca on the Nile, taken by the Mallowans.

Background: The Nile, late twentieth century.

MURDER IN THE MEWS

Murder in the Mews, London: Collins, The Crime Club,1936
Dead Man's Mirror, New York: Dodd, Mead, 1937

Below: A Standard Swallow Saloon car was spotted outside Mrs Allen's flat in the fictional Bardsley Garden Mews. It was traced to a Major Eustace, who becomes chief suspect for her death. This model was only in production between 1931 and 1933.

Background

The year 1937 was a particularly productive one for Christie. In addition to *Death on the Nile*, she published *Dumb Witness* and *Murder in the Mews*, a collection of four Poirot novellas including the title story. The American edition was entitled 'Dead Man's Mirror', after another story in the collection, presumably because the term 'Mews' would not be meaningful to the average American. It contained only three stories, omitting 'The Incredible Theft', possibly on the grounds that it was a reworking of an earlier and much shorter story called 'The Submarine Plans', first published in *The Sketch* in November 1923. This logic did not, however, stop the inclusion of 'Dead Man's Mirror', which was itself an expanded reworking of 'The Second Gong' (later to be published by Dodd in 1948 in a collection entitled *Witness for the Prosecution* and by HarperCollins in 1991 in the collection *Problem at Pollensa Bay)*. All four stories feature Poirot on top form.

Price - - £245

140 • The 1930s

Storyline

The title story begins with Poirot and Japp returning to Poirot's flat after dinner. They take a short cut through Bardsley Garden Mews where next morning a woman is discovered dead from gunshot wounds. Her flatmate was away the previous evening and can offer Japp no assistance. Because both the windows and the door to the room where the woman was found were locked, Japp's initial finding is that the death must have been suicide. But clues emerge to suggest otherwise – the key to the door is missing and part of a cufflink is found as well as an ashtray full of cigarettes.

An interview with the dead woman's fiancé, a particularly pompous MP, elicits more concern for his own reputation than for the dead woman. Japp discovers that the woman had withdrawn a large sum of money the day she died and may have been the victim of a blackmailer. Enquiries lead to a Major Eustace, who admits to having been in the victim's house on the night in question and happens to smoke the same type of cigarettes as those whose remains are found in the ashtray. His broken cufflink matches the piece found in the room and Japp promptly arrests him. Poirot has other ideas and duly confronts his suspect and explains his deductions, which prove correct. The story is most satisfying, although Christie had used her central plot device before. 'The Incredible Theft' is a considerably expanded version of an earlier short story, with the submarine of the earlier title becoming a bomber aircraft. The story benefits from its revision and expansion and ends satisfactorily with the retrieval of the crucial plans by Poirot after a particularly convincing exercise of the little grey cells.

Above left:
The art-deco Florin Court, at Charterhouse Square, London, made a beautiful facade for Poirot's flat in dramatizations.

Above right:
Agatha's own flat in Cresswell Place, London, which she let out in the late 1930s. Nearby are many mews with strikingly similar names to the Bardsley Garden Mews of the book.

MURDER IN THE MEWS

Right: The first edition dustjacket of *Murder in the Mews*, by Robin Macartney again, but quite different in design from the earlier desert novels. The same wrapper is used for a later reprint by Odhams Press, but the spine is plain white with the Odhams logo on the base of the spine.

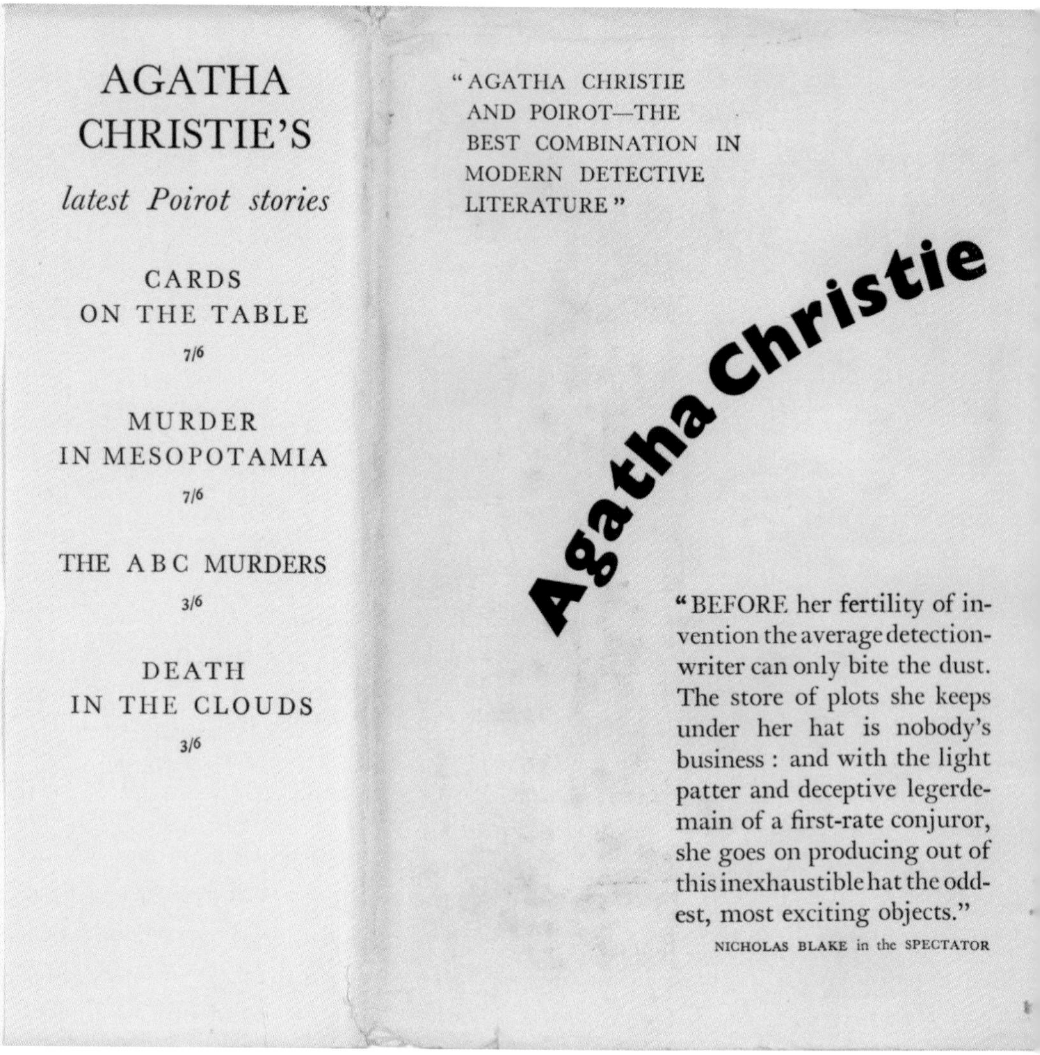

AGATHA CHRISTIE'S

latest Poirot stories

CARDS
ON THE TABLE
7/6

MURDER
IN MESOPOTAMIA
7/6

THE A B C MURDERS
3/6

DEATH
IN THE CLOUDS
3/6

"AGATHA CHRISTIE AND POIROT—THE BEST COMBINATION IN MODERN DETECTIVE LITERATURE"

Agatha Christie

"BEFORE her fertility of invention the average detection-writer can only bite the dust. The store of plots she keeps under her hat is nobody's business : and with the light patter and deceptive legerdemain of a first-rate conjuror, she goes on producing out of this inexhaustible hat the oddest, most exciting objects."

NICHOLAS BLAKE in the SPECTATOR

'Dead Man's Mirror', another highly effective reworking of a much shorter story, marks a return to the classic thriller, with a dead body discovered in the library. There is a splendid collection of suspects present, including Mr Satterthwaite, whom readers may have met earlier in the Harley Quin stories and in *Three-Act Tragedy*. For once, the murderer really does turn out to be the most unlikely of the suspects, but he is no match for Poirot.

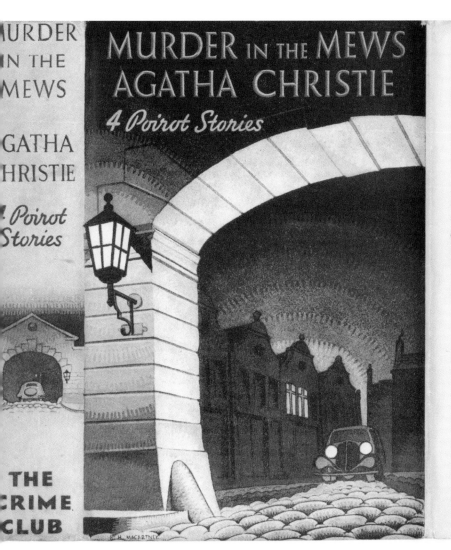

MURDER IN THE MEWS
AGATHA CHRISTIE
4 Poirot Stories

THE CRIME CLUB

THE FOUR long-short Poirot stories in this volume are absolutely first class. Agatha Christie is just as good in a shorter story as she is in a full-length novel, and in these four tales she has devised four more cases to tantalise and entertain us. Or shall we borrow one of Torquemada's witticisms and call them four more "little grey sells!"

7/6 NET

In the last story of the collection, 'Triangle at Rhodes', Poirot, holidaying alone, meets a group of English tourists. One of them, the beautiful Valentine Chantry, is flirting with Douglas Gold, to the annoyance of the former's husband and the latter's wife. Gossip has it that Valentine wishes to divorce her husband and to marry Gold. Unfortunately for her, any such plans are thwarted by her death from a poisoned drink. Valentine's grieving husband

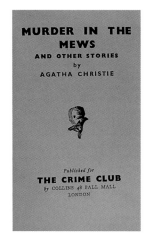

MURDER IN THE
MEWS
AND OTHER STORIES
by
AGATHA CHRISTIE

Published for
THE CRIME CLUB
by COLLINS 48 PALL MALL
LONDON

M.HERCULE POIROT
56B WHITEHAVEN MANSIONS
SANDHURST SQUARE
LONDON WI
TELEPHONE – TRA 8137

Clockwise from top: The UK cloth binding; although as plain as the other late novels, it is surprisingly expensive today; the set of Inspector Japp's office, a delightful evocation of the period by the design team; the fictional address of Monsieur Poirot; the title page of the Collins edition.

The four short stories that make up *Murder in the Mews* still stand as one of the most charming and intriguing set of puzzles Christie devised and evoke a real sense of the period, which makes the book a rare piece for any collection today. Whether one owns an original or not, it is still a pleasure to read and to watch the subsequent TV series.

believes that Gold put poison in the glass and intended it for him. Gold is discovered with poison on him and is immediately arrested. Poirot visits him and is convinced the police have got the wrong man; it is only a matter of time before he identifies the real murderer.

Book Description

The book is a standard demy-octavo volume measuring 198 mm by 128 mm, bound in orange cloth and lettered in black. The text runs from pages 11 to 280 with four pages of publisher's advertisements at the end. The dust-wrapper is once more by Robin Macartney, who shows himself to be as proficient at drawing the metropolis as he is the Middle East. The upper panel shows a typical 1930s mews scene with a magnificent sports car dominating everything, and the spine shows the rear view of the car disappearing into the night.

Reviews

For once the reviews were lukewarm. E. R. Punshon, writing in the *Manchester Guardian,* concluded that it was 'perhaps enough to say that they are all good but not outstanding'. The *Times Literary Supplement* found 'the ideas are not highly original, but to all M. Poirot finds an unexpected solution – in three cases not only unexpected by the reader, but unpredictable'.

Spin-Offs

All four stories were adapted for television in the series starring David Suchet as Poirot, Hugh Fraser as Hastings and Philip Jackson as Inspector Japp. 'Murder in the Mews' and 'Triangle at Rhodes' were first televised on London Weekend Television in 1989; the other two were first shown in 1993, all to the now familiar and much-deserved critical acclaim.

APPOINTMENT WITH DEATH

London: Collins, The Crime Club, 1938
New York: Dodd, Mead, 1938

Background

Opposite: The handsome and timeless columns at Petra, where murder takes place in the novel, providing the glamour and mystery familiar from many Christie novels.

According to Mallowan, writing in the opening paragraph of chapter nine of his memoirs, he and his colleagues were forced to abandon Tell Brak for another site 'over a hundred miles westwards' in the Balikh Valley 'because of the blackmailing pressure of the Sheikhs of the Shammar tribe who were obviously bent on inducing our workmen to strike'. It was to be their last dig in the Middle East before world events conspired to prevent any immediate possibility of return. Their time was spent to good effect, both in terms of archaeological discoveries and Christie's fiction, and they returned to England in December 1938. *Appointment with Death* begins in Jerusalem and moves to Petra, Burgon's 'Rose-red city, half as old as time', with memorable descriptions of both sites as well as the desert wastes of Judaea and the Dead Sea.

Storyline

Against this exotic background, Christie brings to life a colourful and varied group of characters. Most belong to the wealthy but divided Boynton family, who are on holiday touring in the Holy Land. The centre of focus is the unpleasant and devious elderly matriarch Emily Boynton, who dominates the entire family of four children and a daughter-in-law and anyone else who comes into her orbit. Other members of the group who make the excursion to Petra include the American Lady Westholme, 'a big, masterful woman with a rocking-horse face', who has married into the English aristocracy and is also a Member of Parliament. In a manner reminiscent of *Murder in Mesopotamia,* in which Christie had some fun at the expense of the Woolleys, there are some remarkable similarities between 'the much respected and almost universally disliked' Lady Westholme and the real Lady Astor, another American who married into the English aristocracy and became an MP. Fortunately for Christie, the formidable Lady Astor gave no evidence of having noticed any comparisons.

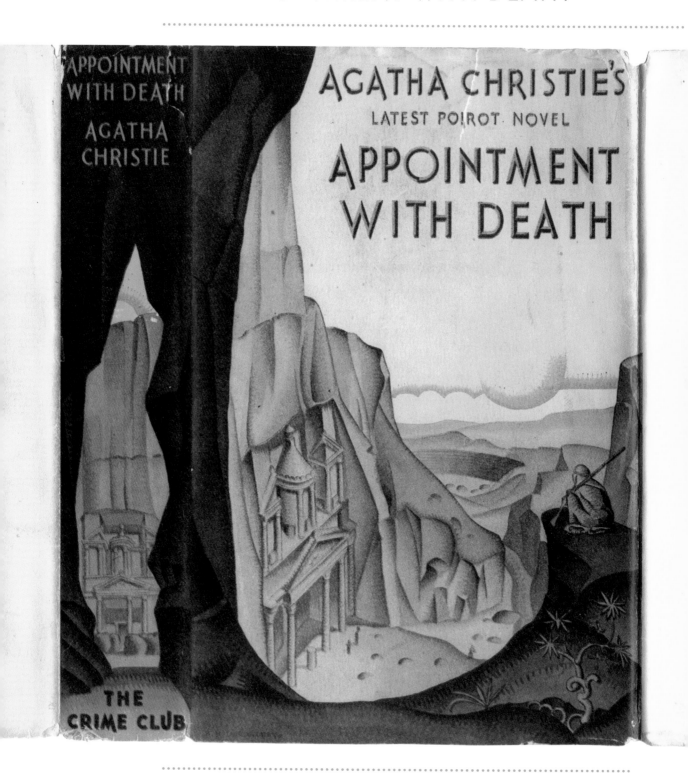

"*You do see, don't you, that she's got to be killed?*" Strange words to float in through a hotel window. Stranger still that Hercule Poirot is the man who overhears them. Later Poirot identifies the voice and his attention is drawn to the Boynton family. Even then he appreciates the psychological forces at work and the terrible emotional strain the Boyntons are undergoing.

We go with them on their journey—from Jerusalem to the Dead Sea and onward into the desert. And there, in the rose red city of Petra, the appointment is kept—with Death. . . .

A perfectly natural death, so it would seem, but Colonel Carbury is worried. He appeals to Poirot who promises him the truth within twenty-four hours. Poirot keeps his word.

7 s. **6** d.
net

Also in the party is a young medical student, a French psychiatrist and, of course, Poirot, who is on holiday but also has an introduction from Colonel Race to a Colonel Carbury who is with the army in Transjordania. When the odious Mrs Boynton is murdered, by a fatal dose of digitoxin injected into her wrist, Poirot is asked to assist in the investigation.

There is, as usual, no shortage of suspects because the late and unlamented victim was not only sadistic but a blackmailer into the bargain. Poirot gets his little grey cells into gear and

Above: A promotional leaflet on flying to Egypt or India from the 1930s.

Opposite: A stunning near full size first edition dustjacket of *Appointment with Death*, by Robin Macartney, which displays his artistic talents to great effect. The jacket is extremely rare in an undamaged state like this.

soon solves the case even allowing the killer a way to avoid further disgrace – another example of Christie's occasional readiness to apply her own justice rather than leave matters to the police and the courts.

Book Description

The book is a standard demy-octavo volume measuring 197 mm by 120 mm; the text runs from pages 9 to 252 with four leaves of publisher's advertisements at the end. It is bound in orange cloth, lettered in black. The dust-wrapper is again by the architect and painter Robin Macartney. The suitably atmospheric and attractive design features on the upper panel a member of a Bedouin tribe, high on a mountain, keeping watch over a valley. The spine features the famous entrance to the temple at Petra.

Reviews

Writing in *The Observer*, Torquemada was generous with his praise, describing the book as 'Twice as brilliant as *Death on the Nile*, which was entirely brilliant.' Praise indeed. The reviewer of the *Yorkshire Post* was similarly impressed, marvelling at 'the superhuman ingenuity of this author'. The *Times* reviewer was less gushing but still managed to refer enthusiastically to 'brilliant deductions'. D. S. Meldrum, writing in the *Daily Telegraph,* was more balanced but could not resist alluding to the characters as 'a brilliantly described group of people'.

Spin-Offs

Christie adapted the book for the stage seven years after the novel had been published. The original title was retained for the play but several significant changes were made, the most noticeable of which was, as before, the omission of Poirot. Back in 1938, in an interview in the *Daily Mail*, Christie had shown signs of irritation with the character of Poirot. 'There are moments when I have felt: Why – why – why did I ever invent this detestable, bombastic, tiresome little creature? ... eternally straightening things, eternally boasting, eternally twirling his moustache and tilting his egg-shaped head.' Whatever the reason – irritation with her character, the lack of suitable actors, or just a feeling that Poirot was not intended for the stage – Christie could not bring herself to produce a stage adaptation which included Poirot. In the play, the investigation of the death of Mrs Boynton was undertaken by Colonel Carbery

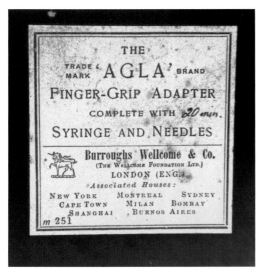

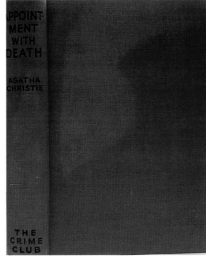

(formerly Carbury), although one of the other characters was to provide the solution. The play has both a different ending from that of the book and a different murderer. After the usual pre-London run, this time in Glasgow, the play opened at the Piccadilly Theatre on 31 March 1945, directed by Terence de Marney.

In 1988, the Cannon Group released the feature version of the book, which happily restored Poirot, played by Peter Ustinov for the third time, along with a stellar cast which included Lauren Bacall as Lady Westholme and Sir John Gielgud as Colonel Carbury. The film was directed by Michael Winner.

Appointment with Death • 151

HERCULE POIROT'S CHRISTMAS

Hercule Poirot's Christmas, London: Collins, The Crime Club,1939
Murder for Christmas, New York: Dodd, Mead, 1939

Background

The blood-red dust-wrapper; the quotation from *Macbeth* – 'Yet who would have thought the old man to have had so much blood in him' – and, above all, the dedicatory letter to her brother-in-law, James Watts, in which Christie refers to his yearning for 'a good violent murder with lots of blood', set the tone for this novel. James Watts' complaint that her murders 'were getting too refined – anaemic in fact' is answered in full in this vintage offering, which brings together two of the favourite devices of the thriller writer of the period, the country-house party and the locked-room murder, to stunning effect.

Storyline

The action takes place between 22 and 28 December in a large country house in the Midlands. The extended family of the wealthy owner, Simeon Lee, a particularly nasty old man, come together for the festive season, not that there is much Christmas cheer about either Gorston Hall or the characters who occupy it. In addition to the old man, who is rumoured to have made his money dishonestly and who never ceases to boast of his infidelities, the permanent inmates of the hall include his son Alfred and the latter's wife Lydia, his sinister manservant Horbury and his aged butler Tressilian. Alfred is very much under his father's thumb, a state of affairs much resented by his wife. Also visiting for Christmas are Simeon's sons Harry, back for the first time since he disappeared with money from a forged cheque; David, gentle and artistic, who hates his father for having been so unpleasant to his late mother, with Hilda his wife, a quiet person of considerable inner strength; and George, a pompous middle-aged MP accompanied by his much younger platinum-blonde wife, Madeleine.

Opposite: Views of Abney Hall in winter, which provided Christie with her setting for murder. Here the Victorian style is ideal for the victim, a successful entrepreneur and businessman. The windows of the fictional Gorston Hall might be a clue in the solving of the bloody murder of Simeon Lee, but the lead is not as straightforward as at first appears. Several puzzling phone calls start Poirot on the trail.

Above: The striking first-edition jacket of *Hercule Poirot's Christmas* with a bright red cover gruesomely suggestive of blood. The later 1930s jackets had large deep front and rear flaps.

The party is completed by two unexpected guests: one Stephen Farr, who presents himself as the son of Ebenezer Farr, a former partner of Simeon's in South Africa, and a beautiful young woman called Pilar Estrevados who is apparently the daughter of Simeon's late daughter Jennifer and who has not previously met her grandfather.

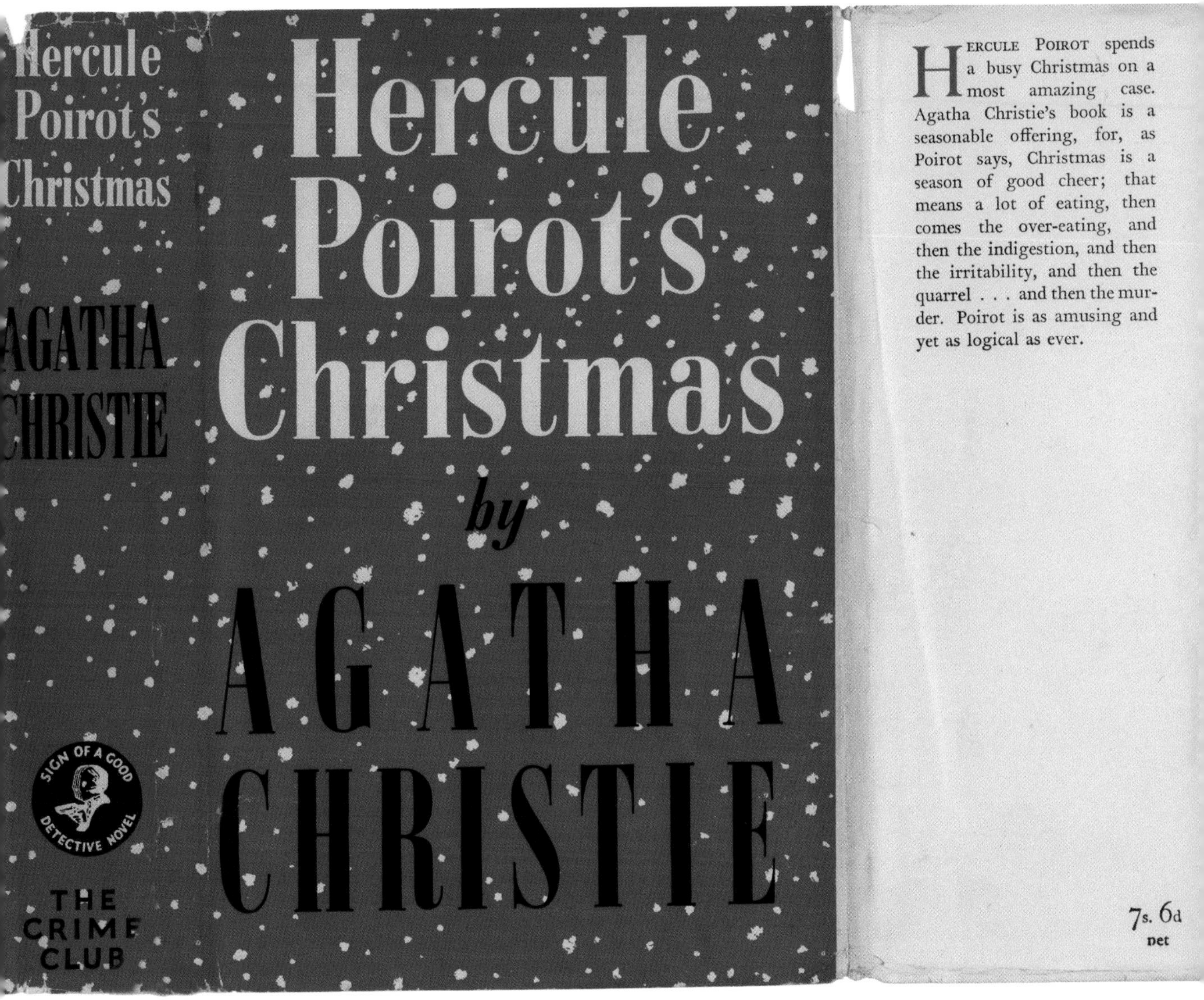
Hercule Poirot's Christmas
AGATHA CHRISTIE
Hercule Poirot's Christmas
by
AGATHA CHRISTIE
SIGN OF A GOOD DETECTIVE NOVEL
THE CRIME CLUB
HERCULE POIROT spends a busy Christmas on a most amazing case. Agatha Christie's book is a seasonable offering, for, as Poirot says, Christmas is a season of good cheer; that means a lot of eating, then comes the over-eating, and then the indigestion, and then the irritability, and then the quarrel . . . and then the murder. Poirot is as amusing and yet as logical as ever.
7s. 6d
net

Tensions among the brothers and their spouses quickly emerge, to be dwarfed by tensions between Simeon and the younger generation, which the old man delights in exacerbating, announcing to the assembled party at one point that he had better sons born on the wrong side of the blanket and publicly summoning his solicitor to attend him on Boxing Day to revise the terms of his will. On Christmas Eve, the old man is murdered.

Top: The drawing room at Abney Hall in 1913, in full pre-war splendour; a similar room is described in *Hercule Poirot's Christmas*. At this time Agatha's sister had just married James Watts.

Below left: The title pages.

Below centre: The first UK cloth-bound edition.

Below right: Another window at Abney Hall, Cheadle, Stockport, yet again providing the inspiration for the plot.

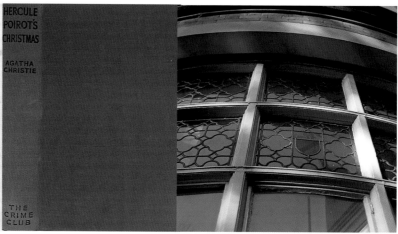

Hearing the crashing of furniture and a long drawn-out scream, the family rush to Simeon's room to find the door locked and, breaking it down, discover the old man lying in a pool of blood with his throat cut. By a remarkable coincidence Police Superintendent Sugden is at the front door, apparently by arrangement to receive a contribution from Simeon for a police charity. He very sensibly telephones the Chief Constable of the county, Colonel Johnson, who is entertaining a former Belgian policeman at that very moment. Poirot is quickly brought into the investigation and in due course apprehends the murderer. The plot is ingenious if far fetched, and it would take an exceptionally cunning reader thoroughly versed in Christie's black arts to identify the murderer – and provide reasons – before Poirot gets there.

Book Description

The book is a standard demy-octavo volume measuring 197 mm by 126 mm. It is bound in orange cloth and lettered in black on the spine. The book consists of 256 pages of which the text runs from pages 11 to 251. The verso of 251 and the next leaf contain reviews of three of Christie's detective stories and the last leaf is blank. The dust-wrapper is a relatively subdued typographical affair with the title in white and the author's name in black on a blood-red background spattered with snowflakes. The pattern is repeated on the spine with the logo of The Crime Club in place above the imprint.

Reviews

Writing in *The Listener*, poet and critic Edwin Muir observed, 'even the corpse is meritorious'. Not all the reviews were reverential. Howard Spring, the novelist, writing in the *Evening Standard,* showed a thorough-going contempt for the book and indeed the oeuvre by revealing the identity and motive of the murderer as well as deconstructing the author's methodology in such a way as to remove any incentive to buy the book or any other Agatha Christie title.

Spin-Offs

As a 1995 New Year's Day treat, London Weekend Television gave a first showing of *Hercule Poirot's Christmas*, with David Suchet turning in his usual immaculate performance as Poirot.

MURDER IS EASY

Murder Is Easy, London: Collins, The Crime Club, 1939
Easy to Kill, New York: Dodd, Mead, 1939

Background and Storyline

The book employs the familiar Superintendent Battle but for once in a minor role and very late in the action. No other familiar characters appear and Battle apart none of the characters reappears. The action takes place in the apparently sleepy village of Wychwood-under-Ashe, a setting redolent of many a Christie triumph. It begins with a chance meeting on a train between Lavinia Pinkerton (renamed Fullerton in the US edition to avoide confusion with the famous detective agency Pinkertons), an old lady from the village, who is on her way to Scotland Yard, and a young man called Luke Fitzwilliam who has just returned to England after several years' policing in the Far East.

It emerges in the course of conversation that Miss Pinkerton is concerned about some unexplained deaths in the village and thinks she can identify the next victim. What might have been dismissed as the ramblings of a dotty old lady are taken seriously when Fitzwilliam reads next day that the old lady has been killed in a hit and run incident. When some days later he reads that the village doctor named as the next victim by Miss Pinkerton has also died, he decides it is time to do some sleuthing. By a remarkable coincidence, his friend Jimmy Lorrimer with whom he is staying, has a cousin, Bridget Conway, who lives in Wychwood. Under cover of researching a book on witchcraft, for which the village is infamous, Fitzwilliam uses Bridget's home as a base for his investigations. The book is an excellent read with Christie's usual array of characters (including a gay antiques dealer, Mr Ellsworthy, who unsurprisingly gets a rough ride), some skilful plotting with delicious red herrings and an exciting finale in which Fitzwilliam gets to the truth before Battle and prevents another murder.

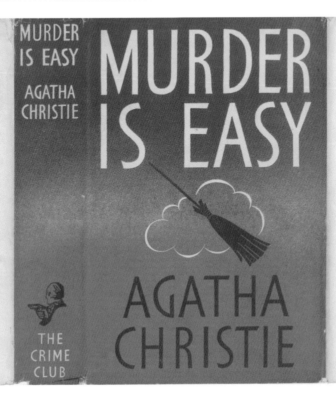

MURDER IS EASY

AGATHA CHRISTIE

THE CRIME CLUB

"Yes, murder," the elderly lady in the railway carriage was saying. "You're surprised, I can see. I was myself, at first. I really couldn't believe it, I thought I must be imagining things. I might have been the first time, but not the second, or the third, or the fourth. After that, one *knows*."

"So many murders!" murmured the other occupant of the railway carriage. (Probably Scotland Yard got half a dozen old ladies a week coming in burbling about the amount of murders committed in their nice quiet country villages. There might be a special department for dealing with the old dears!) "So many murders! Rather hard to do a lot of murders and get away with it, eh?" Miss Pinkerton shook her head. "No, no, my dear boy, *that's* where you're wrong. It's very easy to kill—so long as no one suspects you. And you see, the person in question is just the last person one *would* suspect. . . ."

But is it the last person *you* would suspect. Surely you won't let Agatha Christie fox you again. It would be "again," wouldn't it?

7s. 6d. net

AGATHA CHRISTIE

e greatest genius at invent-
detective-story plots that
r lived or ever will live—
I could prove that too!
true lover of detective
ries would want to miss
book by her."

—PHILIP HEWITT-MYRING in the NEWS CHRONICLE

Book Description

The volume measures 190 mm by 120 mm and consists of 256 pages of which the text runs from pages 9 to 254; the last leaf consists of advertisements. The book is bound in orange cloth lettered in black on the spine. The dust-wrapper is a sober affair with the upper panel and spine in pale olive-green. The upper panel is dominated by the white lettering of the title which is separated from the dark olive of the author's name by a dark olive broomstick against the white outline of a cloud. The spine is lettered in white with the Crime Club gunman in dark olive.

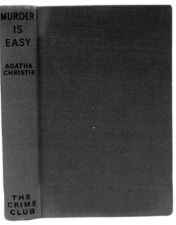

Left: A well-preserved example of the binding of the first UK edition.

AND THEN THERE WERE NONE

Ten Little Niggers, London: Collins, The Crime Club, 1939
And Then There Were None, New York: Dodd, Mead, 1940

Background

The first of several books inspired by nursery rhymes, *And Then There Were None,* is by popular acclaim the best of them and arguably one of Christie's very best books. It was understandably one of her own favourites. In her autobiography, she wrote: 'I had written the book … because it was so difficult to do that the idea had fascinated me. Ten people had to die without it becoming ridiculous or the murderer being obvious. I wrote the book after a tremendous amount of planning, and I was pleased with what I had made of it. It was clear, straightforward, baffling, and yet had a perfectly reasonable explanation…' The original title, acceptable in the England of 1939, was then, as now, unacceptable in the USA and in the 1980s the last few words of the nursery rhyme *And Then There Were None* replaced the opening words as the standard English-language title worldwide.

Storyline

Ten men and women are lured to a solitary house built by an eccentric millionaire on a tiny island off the coast of Devon which is inaccessible except in calm weather. In each bedroom, over the fireplace, hangs a framed copy of the nursery rhyme. One by one, each of the ten guests dies in a way related to the relevant couplet in the nursery rhyme.

The suspense is brilliantly maintained right to the end. Even then, when there are only two characters left, most readers still cannot determine who, if anyone, will be the survivor. In the end, as intended, there is no one left. The solution for the baffled reader lies in an epilogue to which the murderer appends a signature. The novel ends with the words, 'When the sea goes down, there will come from the mainland boats and men. And they will find ten dead bodies and an unsolved problem on Indian Island.'

Background: An aerial view of Burgh Island off the coast of Bigbury-on-Sea, South Devon; the rocky coastline and beaches provided Christie with a perfect setting for the murders. The island had often been used by pirates and smugglers in the past, and the single inn on the island, next to the hotel, was named 'The Pilchards', in association with the numerous mariners who fished and made their livelihoods here.

This page: Aerial and ground views of Burgh Island. The Pilchards Inn, next to the hotel, has been a fixture for many centuries and visitors can still enjoy a refreshing drink there today. The hotel can just be seen in white, at the north side, facing inland.

Ten little Indian boys went out to dine;
One choked his little self and then there were Nine.
Nine little Indian boys sat up very late;
One overslept himself and then there were Eight.
Eight little Indian boys travelling in Devon;
One said he'd stay there and then there were Seven.
Seven little Indian boys chopping up sticks;
One chopped himself in half and then there were Six.
Six little Indian boys playing with a hive;
A bumble bee stung one and then there were Five.
Five little Indian boys going in for law;
One got into Chancery and then there were Four.
Four little Indian boys going out to sea;
A red herring swallowed one and then there were Three.
Three little Indian boys walking in the Zoo;
A big bear hugged one and then there were Two.
Two little Indian boys sitting in the sun;
One got frizzled up and then there was One.
One little Indian boy left all alone;
He went and hanged himself and then there were None.

Opposite above: The rear view of the Burgh Island hotel, depicting the stunning modernist design. The distinctive green Crittall windows always present conservationists with the problem of corrosion, because 1930s metal frames (unlike today's improved models) were not galvanised.

Opposite below: Burgh Island from the mainland, when the tide is low enough to enable visitors to walk across the sands. At high tide, the unique ferry-bus on wheels transports passengers to the island.

Book Description

The British book is a standard demy-octavo, bound in red cloth and lettered in black. It consists of 252 pages, of which the text runs from pages 5 to 252.

Reviews

That Christie had triumphantly achieved the difficult task she had set herself was instantly acknowledged by the critics. The *Observer* considered this 'one of the very best, most genuinely bewildering Christies yet written'. The *Daily Herald* found it 'the most astonishingly impudent, ingenious and altogether successful mystery story for fourteen or fifteen years since *The Murder of Roger Ackroyd*'. The *New Statesman* insisted, 'She stands hors concours, in a class of her own. No one else in the world would have attempted seriously to manipulate a plot like that of *Ten Little Niggers* without a hopeless presentiment of failure. To show her utter superiority over our deductive faculty, Mrs Christie even allows us to know what every character present is thinking and we still can't guess!' On the other side of the Atlantic, *Time* magazine described the book as 'one of the most ingenious thrillers in many a day'.

AND THEN THERE WERE NONE

Above: The first UK edition dust-jacket of *Ten Little Niggers,* as the book was originally named. The rear cover is black with a white box promoting the other titles in a cheaper 2/6 edition. The UK jacket is strikingly offensive by our standards today, but it still demands large sums from collectors.

Right: The US jacket is designed with more flair than the UK version, and correctly uses Burgh Island with a white hotel on the front cover. The hotel depicted is of a neutral and unspecific design, not particularly like the modernist style of the real building.

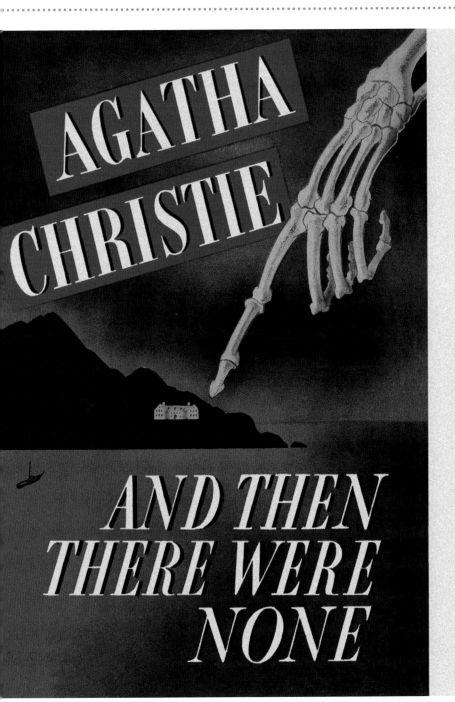

$2.00

AND THEN THERE WERE NONE

By AGATHA CHRISTIE

Author of
THE MURDER OF ROGER ACKROYD

*Ten little Indians went out to dine
One choked his little self and then there were nine.
Nine little Indians . . .*

—so went the nursery rhyme which each guest read with such casual amusement—

*. . . One little Indian left all alone,
He went and hanged himself and then there were none!*

AGATHA CHRISTIE has always shown a genius for the "closed" murder problem, in which the possible suspects are limited to a small and definite group. In this story ten people are invited to a lonely mansion on Indian Island by a host who, surprisingly, fails to appear—ten people each of whom has something to hide, something to fear. On the Island they are cut off by a storm from everything but each other and the inescapable shadows of their own past lives.

Even on the first glorious summer evening there seemed to be something sinister about that Island, but not a one of them suspected then the diabolical series of events that would be set in motion by the Voice after dinner. . . .

AND THEN THERE WERE NONE is unique in a number of ways—it contains no detective, not even an amateur investigator; it is so constructed that it cannot be unfair. Agatha Christie's brilliance has long been established, she has a score of the finest detective stories to her credit, but this one tops everything she has done—here is the perfect murder story, a classic of crime.

DODD, MEAD & COMPANY

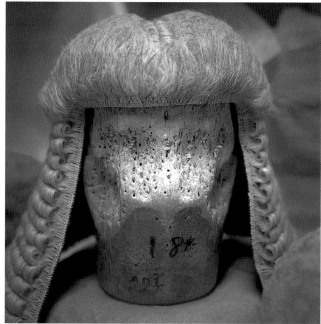

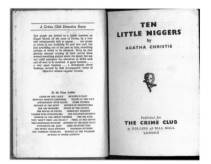

Above left: The first UK cloth-bound edition and the title pages, showing the reversed Crime Club Gunman.

Above right: The wig of the judge 'who got into Chancery'.

Right: An interior of the Burgh Island Hotel today; it is still maintained lovingly by its current owners.

166 • The 1930s

Spin-Offs

As if writing the book had not proved a sufficient challenge, Christie decided she would write a play based on the book. She accepted that her device of an epilogue would not work well on the stage and changed the ending in a way which still had great dramatic effect and was accounted a huge success. The play began with a short run at the Wimbledon Theatre, under the book's original title, before moving to the St James's Theatre in the West End in November 1943. It had a strong cast and was well received by the critics, running until the theatre became a casualty of the Blitz when it was transferred to the Cambridge where it continued for several months. In the summer of 1944, the play, now retitled *Ten Little Indians,* had a very successful New York run. The play was revived in England in 1966 with its original title, but sufficient objection was made to cause its producers hurriedly to introduce the later title.

No fewer than three films of the story have been made, choosing as their text not the novel but the later play. The first, made by Twentieth Century Fox in 1945 under the direction of René Clair, was a great success, not least because it used some of Hollywood's best character actors.

In 1965 Seven Arts Films, with George Pollock as director, made a new version in England. Despite a stellar cast, the film was not well received. Liberties were taken with the setting which was moved to an isolated hotel in the Alps and with some of the characterization, for reasons which were unclear. Ten years later, Avco Embassy made a third version with Peter Collinson as director. Yet more changes were introduced to the characterization in order to accommodate a big-name international cast. The setting was moved again, this time to the Shah Abah Hotel in Isfahan in Iran. The critics, including Christie, were vociferous in their denunciation of the film.

Following page left: Flying into Burgh Island, a world apart from the mainland. Hovering right over the island, one can see the white art-deco hotel that appeared in *And Then There Were None* and *Evil Under the Sun.*

Following page right: The sunset off Burgh Island, from the shore.

The 1940s

ONE, TWO, BUCKLE MY SHOE

One, Two, Buckle My Shoe, London: Collins, The Crime Club, 1940
The Patriotic Murders, New York: Dodd, Mead, 1940

Background

The year 1940 produced a second Poirot novel, following closely on the heels of *Sad Cypress* (placed following this chapter due to constraints on space). This time, the title came not from Shakespeare but from the first line of a children's nursery rhyme, which is quoted in full before the text of the story begins and provides a structure for it with each of the ten lines of doggerel corresponding roughly to one of the book's ten chapters. Nursery rhymes were to figure strongly as inspiration for several Christie novels: triumphantly in *And Then There Were None* and to greater or lesser effect in others. Her US publishers, perhaps uncertain of American readers' knowledge of this particular rhyme, decided to change the title and let their readers work it all out without benefit of the literary subtext, a decision which if the reviews were anything to go by was entirely justified.

The title chosen by Dodd was by no means inappropriate. This story does not hark back to a gentler and more settled period but is full of references to current affairs. Although the war itself is unmentioned, there are references to Hitler and Mussolini, to Mosley's Fascists, to the threat of Communism and to the IRA. For its 1953 paperback edition, the American publisher Dell chose the slightly camp and self-referential title *An Overdose of Death*, which provides a critical commentary on the book itself and indeed on the genre as a whole.

Opposite above: A post-theatre party for the British in full swing, in 1928. In the hot weather, the clothing is rapidly moving towards a softer, more fluid line.

Opposite below: The murder's original starting point in India, here illustrated in full Raj style in 1928, twelve years before the murders began.

Storyline

The opening chapter begins with a fashionable London dentist, one Henry Morley, complaining to his sister-housekeeper about his breakfast, the government, the fact that his secretary had been called away to a sick relative, the uncouth manners of the

new door-boy and the very busy morning that lies ahead of him. Successive sections introduce us to his patients, who include one Hercule Poirot, who is in mortal fear of his six-monthly dental appointment. Poirot survives the attentions of the dentist only to discover later in the day in the course of a phone call from the redoubtable Inspector Japp that Morley has been found dead in his surgery and, later on, that one of the morning's other patients, the mysterious Mr Amberiotis, has been found dead in his hotel room apparently from an overdose of dental anaesthetic. The inquest finds that Morley killed himself having realized that he accidentally killed his patient. As any Christie aficionado will instinctively suspect, Japp's conclusion is wrong.

Above: The set created for the late 1930s surgery of Mr Morley, the first victim, for London Weekend Television; here Rob Harris and Carlotta Barrow recreate the look with superb attention to detail.

Opposite: Fashionable shoes from about 1928, which by 1940 were no longer la mode. The third victim, a Miss Sainsbury Seale, yet another patient of Mr Morley, is found dead with these distinctive shoes on, reflecting her slightly dowdy style of dress. Poirot is puzzled by the discrepancies between the stockings and the shoes and her disfigured face. Yet it is the buckled shoes that provide him with the clue to solving one of his most challenging murder cases.

ONE, TWO, BUCKLE MY SHOE

Recent Successes by

Agatha Christie

★

SAD CYPRESS

"Agatha Christie has done it again, which is all you need to know." OBSERVER

★

TEN LITTLE NIGGERS

"Ranks with Agatha Christie's previous best, on the top-notch of detection" NEW STATESMAN

★

MURDER IS EASY

"I should hate to have to state on oath which I thought was Agatha Christie's best story, but I can say that this is well up in the first six." OBSERVER

AGATHA CHRISTIE

" the greatest genius

at inventing

detective story plots

that ever lived

or

ever will live "

—NEWS CHRONICLE

Above: The first UK dust-jacket, now using a darker colour scheme with the onset of war. The books move with the times, in content and appearance. This was the turning point; the base colour is always difficult to define, but appears on original copies to be a subtle mixture of purple and brown. The slanting typeface always makes a refreshing contribution and is a common feature of the 1940s jackets.

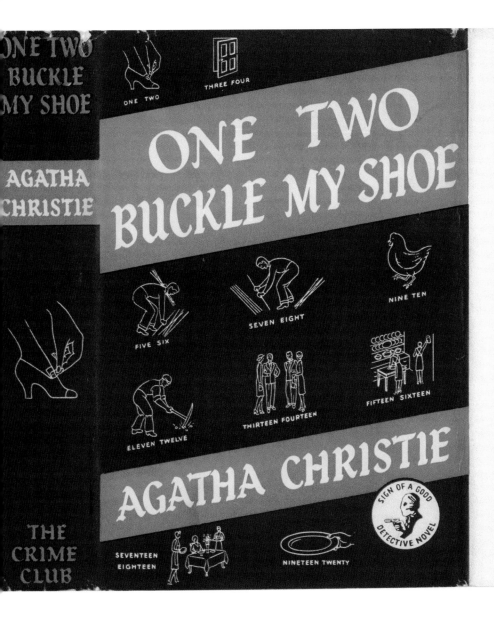

It has been said that no man is a hero to his valet. To that may be added that few men are heroes to themselves at the moment of visiting their dentist. Hercule Poirot was, says Mrs. Christie, "morbidly conscious of this fact" as he entered his dentist's room in Queen Charlotte Street. "His morale was down to zero. He was just that ordinary, that craven figure, a man afraid of the dentist's chair."

For the reader it is a very pleasant turning of the tables to see the great Poirot at such a disadvantage, his mouth stuffed with cotton wool, hot air puffing down the cavity, unable to speak for himself! At half-past eleven Poirot stepped out, a free man. But before lunch-time sudden death had claimed a victim at the dentist's. Soon Poirot was probing into the integrity of his fellow patients of that morning. The problem into which he is led provides him with one of his best cases.

7s. 6d.
net

Above: The first US jacket of *One, Two, Buckle My Shoe,* here titled *The Patriotic Murders,* with a pleasing bold design and a good use of colour. American designs generally used vivid colours which reflected the availability of colour pigments and paper before the effects of war took hold.

Below left: A period hypodermic needle set.

Below right: The title pages; the book was bound in plain red as before with a blank front board.

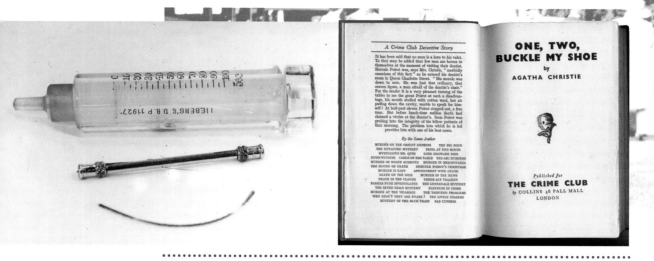

Christie maintains a tight grip on a complicated plot, which involves blackmail and dual identity in addition to murder. A further murder is discovered and hitherto unknown connections between those who attended the dentist on that fateful morning are gradually unearthed. Enlightenment eventually comes to Poirot in the course of morning service in the village church which he is dutifully attending with his host, an important banker and one of Poirot's fellow dental patients. Following through this revelatory line of thought, he is rewarded in due course by the murderer's confession.

Book Description

The book is a standard demy-octavo in the usual red cloth lettered in black. It consists of 256 pages of which the text runs from pages 9 to 252. The remaining printed pages advertise new Crime Club publications and Agatha Christie titles available in the Uniform 2/6 Edition and invite non-members to join the club. The Crime Club gunman motif is present, facing left, on the title page but not on the spine, which contains title, author and imprint only. The upper and lower covers are plain. The green and brown dust-wrapper is built up with motifs which allude to the nursery rhyme of the title.

Reviews

The book did not receive unalloyed praise. Fairly typical was the review in the *New York Times* of 2 March 1940, which read: 'It's a real Agatha Christie thriller: exceedingly complicated plot, briskly simple in narrative, with a swift course of unflagging suspense that leads to complete surprise. After closing the book one may murmur "far-fetched" or even "impossible". But any such complaint will be voiced only after the story has been finished; there won't be a moment to think of such things before.'

Spin-Offs

In 1992, London Weekend Television filmed *One, Two, Buckle My Shoe*, directed by Ross Devenish. David Suchet played Poirot for the thirty-third time and Philip Jackson played Chief Inspector Japp for the twenty-ninth time. This was another fine production with exemplary technical credits and the wonderful evocation of period atmosphere which viewers of this series have come to expect.

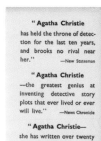
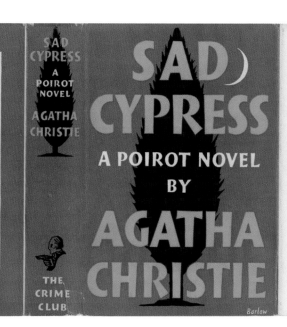

Above: The UK 1940 jacket for *Sad Cypress* exhibits a confident design. The background is an unusual shade of blue-green, which together with a bold use of typeface creates an entirely new style for Christie's book covers. The cheap editions are promoted on the rear cover.

Below: The red cloth binding of *N or M?* has a reversed question mark on the spine and a reversed Crime Club gunman on the title page. The jacket here is very different from previous designs, being finished in soft shaded pastel colours, lending a slightly romantic air. However it is still recognizable as a typically 1940s piece of artwork.

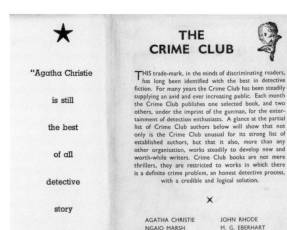
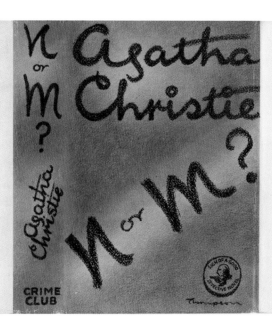

Sad Cypress and **N or M?**

Sad Cypress
London: Collins, The Crime Club, 1940; New York: Dodd, Mead, 1940

The book opens dramatically, with Elinor Carlisle on trial for the murder of Mary Gerrard, with whom her ex-fiancé had fallen in love. Poirot is in court and takes on the difficult task of saving her from the hangman in what appears to be an open and shut case, in which the victim died from poisoning after eating sandwiches prepared for her by Elinor. Many years later Christie was to state that the book was ruined by the presence of Poirot. But opinions differ on this point; the book works well as a murder mystery and had Christie seen the televisation with David Suchet as Poirot, she might have changed her mind. The volume measures 190 by 125 mm and consists of 256 pages of which the text occupies pages 7 to 252, the last leaves being advertisements. The upper panel of the dust-wrapper is basically typographical with yellow-ochre lettering over a black cypress tree on an aquamarine background with a white new moon and 'A Poirot novel by' also in white between author and title. A miniature version appears on the spine with the Crime Club lettering in white at the foot and the gunman in black above.

N or M?
London: Collins, The Crime Club, 1941; New York: Dodd, Mead, 1941

In her autobiography, written many years later, Christie confessed to writing *N or M?* and *The Body in the Library* at the same time 'to keep her fresh at the task'. She saw the former, featuring a middle-aged Tommy and Tuppence, as a continuation of *The Secret Adversary*, with the pair tracking down spies 'with all their old enthusiasm', as anxious to contribute to the war effort as their children: Deborah code-breaking and Derek in the RAF. The Beresfords have been asked by the Secret Service to assist in the capture of a group of Fifth Columnists and leap at the opportunity. Albert Batt, first encountered as a lift-boy in *The Secret Adversary* and now running a public house in Kennington, is keen to help, and this somewhat unlikely trio set out to foil the enemy, which they do triumphantly after some hair-raising adventures and near-disasters. The volume consists of 192 pages of which the text occupies pages 5 to 192. There are no advertisement leaves. The book is bound in orange cloth lettered in black on the spine. The dust-wrapper is a subdued typographical affair in keeping with wartime restrictions.

EVIL UNDER THE SUN

London: Collins, The Crime Club, 1941
New York: Dodd, Mead, 1941

Background

Christie at this time was putting in three half-days and alternate Saturday mornings in the dispensary at London's University College Hospital and filling in additionally for any other members of the dispensing staff who had been prevented from turning up for work by the bombing. Writing thus became an evening activity, which was probably sensible in a blacked-out and blitzed London in which simply being resident was dangerous enough. Perhaps there was an element of wish fulfilment in having Poirot take a few days' holiday from London to stay in a highly select hotel off the coast of her beloved Devon.

Storyline

Away from the London of the Blitz, Poirot soon relaxes, but not to the extent that he cannot observe the possibilities for murder presented by the mix of guests and the location of his hotel with its extensive grounds, which becomes an island inaccessible from the mainland, when the tide is in. It soon becomes clear that a murder is inevitable and Poirot, somewhat complacently, sits back waiting for it to happen.

The victim, who is widely disliked, is clearly marked and there are few mourners when she is killed. At the heart of the matter is an emotional triangle which is reminiscent of some others in the Christie oeuvre. The principals are as always well characterized and there is no shortage of motive or opportunity.

Opposite above: The classic art-deco interior of the Burgh Island Hotel, with the characteristic Lloyd Loom chairs. This area is now called Palm Court. Thankfully the building retains all of its original features, such as the distinctive Crittall-style windows, that give it such an elegant appearance.

Opposite below: Burgh Island from the mainland at low tide, revealing the marks of the tractor that transports travellers to the island and the famous hotel.

Evil under the Sun • 181

EVIL UNDER THE SUN

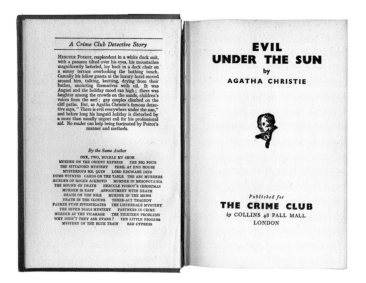 

Christie has some fun with an American couple, which cannot have commended itself to her American readership but which is harmless enough. The presence of the Chief Constable of the county provides at one and the same time an interesting line in suspects and an opportunity for Poirot to demonstrate the superiority of his little grey cells. It goes without saying that it is Poirot who solves the murder and not the senior policeman.

Book Description

The book is a standard demy-octavo volume. It measures 190 mm by 125 mm and consists of 256 pages, of which the text occupies pages 9 to 252 with three pages of advertisements; page 256 is blank. It is bound in plain orange cloth with black lettering on the spine in the usual title – author – imprint order. The Crime Club gunman is present on the title page, facing left as usual. The dust-wrapper, which is unpriced on the spine, has a stylish and indeed stylised design by Rose featuring rocks and sea under a high hot sun. The spine and upper panel are integrated into the design, leaving the lower panel free for book promotion.

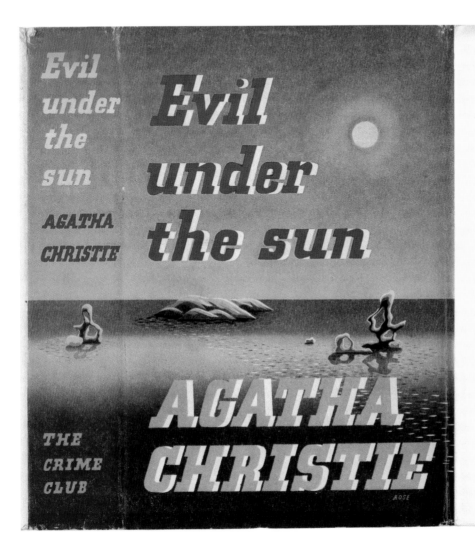

Evil under the sun

AGATHA CHRISTIE

THE CRIME CLUB

Evil under the sun

AGATHA CHRISTIE

HERCULE POIROT, resplendent in a white duck suit, with a panama tilted over his eyes, his moustaches magnificently befurled, lay back in a deck chair on a sunny terrace overlooking the bathing beech. Casually his fellow guests at the luxury hotel moved around him, talking, knitting, drying from their bathes, anointing themselves with oil. It was August and the holiday mood ran high; there was laughter among the crowds on the sands, children's voices from the surf; gay couples climbed on the cliff paths. But, as Agatha Christie's famous detective says, "there is evil everywhere under the sun," and before long his languid holiday is disturbed by a more than usually urgent call for his professional aid. No reader can help being fascinated by Poirot's manner and methods.

7s. 6d. net

Above: The first UK dust-jacket. This is one of the prettier jackets from the 1940s, with its mysterious sunset and colouring of the front cover and spine. In contrast to the handwritten style used for many of Christie's covers at this time, the typeface has a modern feel which is reminiscent of the 1950s Pan paperbacks. The slant gives the title a sense of urgency and dash, an effect also seen in earlier publications such as *The Listerdale Mystery* and later ones such as *The Moving Finger.*

Above: The private beach near the hotel, off the island, is here set for murder as the boat awaits the return of Arlena Stuart, who is later found strangled. The clock and a wristwatch provide alibis for a number of suspects.

Left: Beachwear in 1940; the swimsuit and dress that the victim Arlena wore in the TV drama, designed by Charlotte Holdich, remain faithful to the period, which for the film version was backdated to the middle to late 1930s.

Reviews

With hindsight, this was not among the very best of Christie's stories, but the book was nevertheless well received on publication. The *Daily Telegraph* gushed patriotically that its author 'had never written anything better than *Evil under the Sun* which is detective story writing at its best'. The *Sunday Chronicle,* not to be outdone, assured its readers that Christie was 'still the best of all detective story writers'. The *Sunday Times* introduced a slightly contentious note when it advised its readers that the book was 'as gratifying as anything that peace-time standards could require', adding, in case anyone might think this comment less than enthusiastic, that 'her characters are vivacious and entertaining'. The *Times Literary Supplement* noted that 'it will take a lot of beating', adding topically to this less than ecstatic judgement that 'she springs her secret like a land-mine'.

Spin-Offs

In 1981, the book was filmed by the team who had made *Murder on the Orient Express, Death on the Nile* and *The Mirror Crack'd from Side to Side*. It was released by EMI Films the following year. Certain changes were made to the plot and to the setting, which was moved from Devon to the Adriatic. It had, as previously, a star-studded cast including Peter Ustinov, who had also played Poirot in *Death on the Nile*. A rather more satisfactory version with the original setting restored to brilliant effect was later made by LWT with David Suchet as Poirot.

THE BODY IN THE LIBRARY

London: Collins, The Crime Club, 1942
New York: Dodd, Mead, 1942

Background

In wartime Britain, away from the exotic Middle Eastern locations which had lent themselves so effectively to the exploits of that seasoned traveller Hercule Poirot, Christie revived the character of Jane Marple, at home in her beloved village of St Mary Mead. Twelve years had passed since Jane Marple had made her debut in *The Murder at the Vicarage* and it was perhaps high time that her readers had a change from Poirot who had figured large in her 1930s output for understandable reasons. Christie, looking back, thought there were too many characters in her first Jane Marple book, but it was good for the continuity of village life that some characters were to recur in this and later Marple stories.

The title, something of a cliché of detective fiction, had been bestowed by Christie in *Cards on the Table* on an earlier imaginary work by a fictional character, Mrs Ariadne Oliver. Six years on, Christie was to use the title to brilliant effect in what is acknowledged to be one of her best detective stories and a triumphant return for Jane Marple.

Opposite above: Abney Hall as ever provides inspiration of this most classic of murders, in which the library is the final destination of the first victim.

Opposite below: An aerial view of the small villages of Devon, which always give Christie's novels such an attractive background setting.

The Body in the Library • 187

Right: The library at Abney Hall is lavishly and exotically decorated, rather more elaborate than the shabby tweedy country style of the Bantrys.

Below: Dunster village in Somerset, pictured in 1940, is a classic English village of the type that appears in Christie's Miss Marple novels. Dunster was also used for filming *The Cornish Mystery*.

Storyline

The story opens at Gossington Hall in the village of St Mary Mead. Dolly Bantry, wife of Colonel Bantry, principal magistrate of the district, has been enjoying a pleasant early-morning dream while vaguely aware that the household is beginning its daily routine around her. She is anticipating the opening of her curtains as prelude to her early morning cup of tea, but she is in for a rude awakening. The knock on her door was followed not by the arrival of tea but by the news, delivered by a hysterical maid, that a body had been found in the library. An outraged Bantry phones the police to report the discovery and Dolly phones her friend Jane who is 'so good at bodies'. The police discover that the body is that of a Ruby Keene, a dance hostess, reported missing from the Majestic Hotel in Danemouth, 'a large and fashionable watering-place' on the coast not far away. The action moves from the hall to the coast, but not before Basil Blake, a young man connected with the film industry and with a cottage in St Mary Mead and a reputation for fast living, has been put in the frame. At the Majestic, interest focuses on Conway Jefferson, who was badly injured in a flying accident that killed his wife, son and daughter. He is looked after by a faithful valet, his daughter-in-law and his son-in-law. But he had developed an affection for Ruby Keene, whom he wished to adopt.

In a further complication, a Girl Guide has gone missing and a body in Guide uniform is discovered in a burnt-out car abandoned in a nearby quarry. Jane Marple seizes on one of the missing Guide's friends, who confesses that the girl had run off to meet a film producer who wanted to give her a screen test. Suspicion again falls on Basil Blake, who is promptly arrested by the police. Jane Marple, however, knows better. She prevents the murder of Conway Jefferson and identifies those responsible for the crimes. She beats the Chief Constable, a superintendent from the neighbouring force and a retired commissioner of Scotland Yard to the truth because she pays attention to apparently trifling matters which the professionals, all men, fail to understand and, above all, because, as she says modestly at one point, 'one does see so much evil in a village'.

Left: Late 1930s dress fashions and dance shoes suitable for Ruby Keene, the first victim.

THE BODY IN THE LIBRARY

Also by
AGATHA CHRISTIE

●

N or M?

"Here is excellent entertainment with a pretty puzzle for any who take their fun seriously."
SUNDAY TIMES

EVIL UNDER THE SUN

"Mrs. Christie is even more ingenious than usual in her discovery of new fool-proof methods of murder."
SPECTATOR

ONE, TWO, BUCKLE MY SHOE

"Mrs. Christie's skill is that of a conjuror: her characters alone would make a book."
SKETCH

THE CRIME CLUB

THIS trade-mark, in the minds of discriminating readers, has long been identified with the best in detective fiction. For many years the Crime Club has been steadily supplying an avid and ever increasing public. Each month the Crime Club publishes one selected book, and two others, under the imprint of the gunman, for the entertainment of detection enthusiasts. A glance at the partial list of Crime Club authors below will show that not only is the Crime Club unusual for its strong list of established authors, but that it also, more than any other organisation, works steadily to develop new and worth-while writers. Crime Club books are not mere thrillers, they are restricted to works in which there is a definite crime problem, an honest detective process, with a credible and logical solution.

AGATHA CHRISTIE	JOHN RHODE
NGAIO MARSH	M. G. EBERHART
RUPERT PENNY	REX STOUT
LESLIE FORD	ANTHONY GILBERT
G. D. H. & M. COLE	HERBERT ADAMS
ANTHONY ABBOT	E. C. R. LORAC
MILES BURTON	NICHOLAS BLAKE

Above: The dust-jacket, unpriced for the foreign market, with its dramatic black background and the bold use of line to create the title, is designed to catch a buyer's eye instantly. The black and red continue the wartime feel of these jackets, with darker colours and a strong design.

Right: A detail at full size.

THE
BODY
IN THE
LIBRARY

AGATHA
CHRISTIE

THE
CRIME
CLUB

by

AGATHA
CHRISTIE

COLONEL and Mrs. Bantry had always believed that "a body in the library" only happened in books—until the day when a body was found in their own library! Whose body was it? Who placed it there? Why should it be found in the library of Gossington Hall? That gentle elderly spinster, Miss Marple (whom readers of Agatha Christie will remember) was faced with all these questions. Following the trail from the quiet village of St. Mary Mead to a fashionable seaside hotel, she eventually found the answer. How did she manage it? Well, in her own words: "It reminded me of Tommy Bond and our new schoolmistress. She went to wind up the clock and a frog jumped out!"

BODY
IN THE
LIBRARY

Clockwise from top: Abney Hall's library from the opposite end, revealing other furnishings and opulent gothic decoration, not to mention a very fine chandelier; the US jacket, which favours the slanted type and, like the UK design, uses black and a darker colour palette for effect; a section of the cloth binding and title of the UK edition.

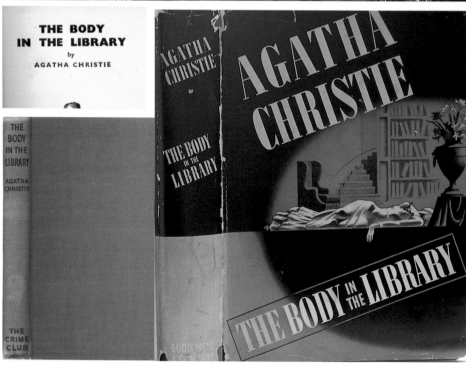

Book Description

The book is a standard demy-octavo volume measuring 190 mm by 120 mm. It consists of 160 pages of which the text runs from pages 7 to 160. There are no advertisement leaves. This is a wartime production and while the story is a triumph, the book shows signs of wartime paper rationing with its smaller format and reduced length. The dust-wrapper by Leslie Stead is simple in concept but striking. On a black background, the title lettering on the upper panel is picked out in blood red against the white outlines of books on library shelves. The author's name on the upper panel and the spine lettering and Crime Club logo are in white.

Reviews

The reviewer in *John O'London's Weekly* found that 'Mrs Christie is an adept at surprise endings … She has one of the nicest of detectives, Miss Marple, to solve the mystery.' The *Observer* commented, 'Ingenious, of course.'

Spin-Offs

The Body in the Library was the first of a series of televisations of all twelve Miss Marple books. The first episode of three was shown on BBC television on Boxing Day 1984. Miss Marple was played throughout the series by Joan Hickson, to the delight of Agatha Christie who regarded her performance as definitive, a conclusion gratefully endorsed by the viewer.

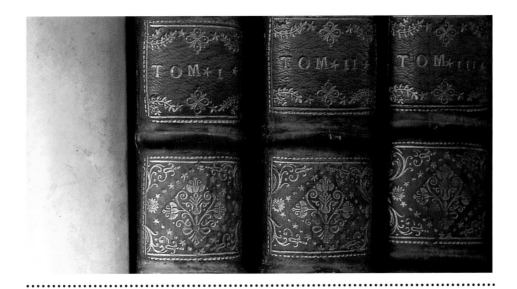

Five Little Pigs and The Moving Finger

Five Little Pigs, London: Collins, The Crime Club, 1942
Murder in Retrospect, New York: Dodd, Mead, 1942

The title of the US edition is more apposite, since the murder concerned was committed sixteen years before the book opens. Caroline Crale died in prison after being found guilty of the murder of her husband, who had fallen in love with another woman and wanted a divorce. But her daughter, now in her twenties, is anxious to clear her mother's name and Poirot is happy to assist. He interviews the five surviving main suspects – the five little pigs – and persuades each to write his or her recollection of the events in question. The variations in the recollections and in the personalities of the five then and now are acutely observed and make for an unusual and absorbing story, although the nursery-rhyme theme is inappropriate. The solution is satisfying if bleak: Caroline Crale's name is cleared and the real murderer identified, although probably too late for prosecution. The book was well reviewed and was the first of Christie's titles to achieve a sale of 20,000 copies at its original price.

Christie later adapted the book for the stage, replacing Poirot with Miss Crale's solicitor, and changing the title to *Go Back for Murder*. After opening in Edinburgh, it moved to London in March 1960. Despite an impressive cast the play closed after just thirty-one performances. The volume measures 190 mm by 120 mm and consists of 192 pages, of which the text occupies pages 9 to 192. The book is bound in orange cloth with the spine lettered in black. The upper panel and spine are in brilliant yellow with lettering and line drawings of nursery-rhyme pigs in pink.

The Moving Finger
New York: Dodd, Mead, 1942; London: Collins, The Crime Club, 1943

Poison-pen letters are threatening the tranquillity of the olde-worlde village of Lymstock. When two deaths occur, one a supposed suicide, the second clearly murder, the vicar's wife Maud Dane Calthrop invites her friend Jane Marple to stay at the vicarage in the hope that she can succeed in solving the murder where the local constabulary has failed.

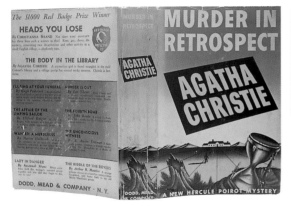

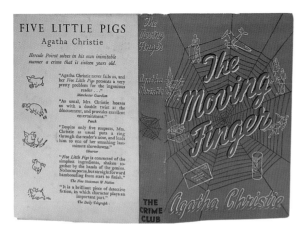

Above left: The US jacket, titled *Murder in Retrospect.* The design is not as strong, but the title works well and reveals more about the nature of the plot.

Above right: The UK jacket of *Five Little Pigs.* The bright yellow gives it a more cheerful appearance, perhaps intended to give relief from the war.

Left: The dust-jacket for *The Moving Finger,* with its striking slanted typeface.

The story is told by Jerry Burton, a young flier who has taken a house locally with his sister to recuperate after a flying accident. Like many another villager he and his sister become victims of the letter-writer, who suggests that his relationship with Joanna is not what it seems. Christie in her autobiography mentions this book as one she was 'really pleased with' and it is a conclusion most readers will share.

The volume measures 190 mm by 125 mm and consists of 160 pages of which the text occupies pages 5 to 160. The upper panel and spine of the dust-wrapper feature a cobweb and red typography in the style of handwriting with black outlining to the upper edge of the letters and white to the lower, on a bright green background. In the cobweb are trapped drawings of people and objects involved in the story. The spine contains the same lettering in miniature, an unadorned cobweb and the imprint, both printed in black.

Towards Zero and Death Comes as the End

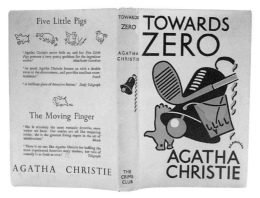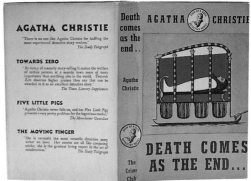

Towards Zero

London: Collins, The Crime Club; New York: Dodd, Mead, 1944

This marks the fifth and final appearance of Superintendent Battle, who for once cannot call on Poirot and has to work hard to solve the murder of Lady Tresillian. This is a tightly plotted murder mystery and study in psychopathic personality set in a beautiful country house overlooking the sea. The book measures 190 mm by 120 mm and consists of 160 pages. It is bound in orange cloth, lettered in black. The bold dust-wrapper features a collage of items all associated with the murder.

In the same year Christie published *Absent in the Spring*, under the pseudonym Mary Westmacott, a novel with strong ties to the Middle East and travel, reflecting her own experiences. It was a favourite of hers and the critics were generous and very enthusiastic about the book.

Death Comes as the End

New York: Dodd, Mead, 1944; London: Collins, The Crime Club, 1945

In this groundbreaking novel, Christie anticipated the modern popularity of historical detective stories by setting her murder plot in ancient Egypt. Much research went into the writing with every chapter scrutinised by a leading Egyptologist, Professor Stephen Glanville, who changed the projected ending against Christie's better judgement. However not even a murder count of eight makes this more than an interesting experiment. The book measures 190 mm by 120 mm and consists of 160 pages. It is bound in orange cloth, lettered in black. The dust-wrapper, printed in gold, blue and grey, features an ancient Egyptian funeral barge being towed down the Nile.

Sparkling Cyanide and **The Hollow**

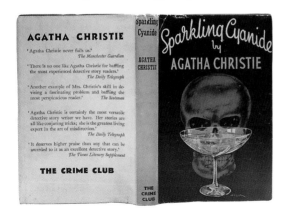 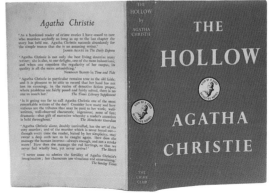

Remembered Death, New York: Dodd, Mead, 1945
Sparkling Cyanide, London: Collins, The Crime Club, 1945

Rosemary Barton dies at a dinner party in a London restaurant after swallowing a poisoned drink. One year on, her grieving husband invites the same guests to an anniversary dinner in the hope that some event will occur which will overturn the official verdict of suicide. That event, unfortunately, is a second murder. The book proved a great success and sold 30,000 copies in its first year. The volume measures 190 mm by 120 mm and consists of 160 pages, with no advertisements at the back. It is bound in orange cloth, lettered in black. The striking dust-wrapper features a green skull grinning through a glass of cyanide-laced champagne.

The Hollow
New York: Dodd, Mead, 1946; London: Collins, The Crime Club, 1946

(Reprinted as *Murder After Hours.*) The action begins with Poirot arriving for a luncheon party at 'The Hollow', the home of his neighbour, Lady Angkatell, to discover his host and other guests by the swimming pool, their attention focused on a woman holding a revolver standing over a dying man. Poirot suspects some infantile joke at his expense, but he is quite wrong. The book proved highly popular, outselling *Sparkling Cyanide* by 10,000 copies. The volume measures 190 mm by 120 mm and consists of 279 pages. It is bound in orange cloth, lettered in black. The dust-wrapper is typographical with white lettering on a red background. Christie's non-fiction account of archaeology, *Come Tell Me How You Live,* was published the same year and was very successful.

Above left: Sparkling Cyanide has an attractive design, with the slightly obvious use of the poisoned glass and a skull on the front. The spine is rather lacking in spark, but the type all over the jacket is very artistic, using the typeface Ashley Crawford on the rear cover, as for *Death Comes as the End.*

Above right: The Hollow is rather plain in contrast, but survives well.

The Labours of Hercules and Taken at the Flood

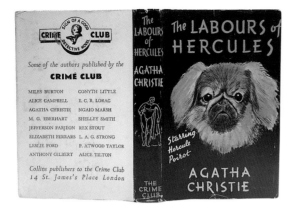 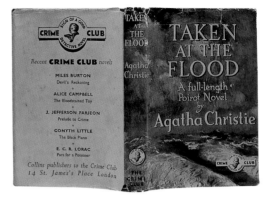

The Labours of Hercules
London: Collins, The Crime Club, 1947; New York: Dodd, Mead, 1947

The collection consists of an account of each of the twelve cases Poirot has decided to take on before his planned retirement, in emulation of his heroic namesake. The first, 'The Nemean Lion', involves the kidnapping, not of a fierce lion but of Shan Tung, a lion-hearted Peke. The collection is very successful with Poirot on excellent form, a high standard of narration overall and clever connections between the ancient world and the modern. The volume measures 190 mm by 120 mm and consists of 256 pages. It is bound in orange cloth, lettered in black. The dust-wrapper features the green head of a Pekingese against a black background. Another Mary Westmacott was published the same year, *The Rose and the Yew Tree*, set in St Loo, Cornwall like *Peril at End House* (1932). It was one of Max Mallowan's favourites.

There is a Tide, New York: Dodd, Mead, 1948
Taken at the Flood, London: Collins, The Crime Club, 1948

The story is set in a post-war Britain in which euphoria has turned to discontent even among the landed gentry. The Cloade family fortunes are in the hands of an attractive young widow following the death of Gordon Cloade, her second husband. When Poirot is visited by Gordon's sister-in-law claiming that the widow's first husband is alive, the stage is set for an exciting drama. The volume measures 190 mm by 120 mm and consists of 192 pages. It is bound in orange cloth, lettered in black. The dust-wrapper features rough seas and stormy skies, alluding to Brutus's speech in Act IV of *Julius Caesar,* from which the title is taken.

Crooked House and A Murder is Announced

Crooked House

London: Collins, The Crime Club, 1949; New York: Dodd, Mead, 1949

The title comes from the nursery rhyme which begins: 'There was a crooked man …'. The little crooked house in the rhyme turns out to be a large crooked house in which three generations of the Leonides family live. The wealthy head of the family is murdered and suspicion falls on the whole household. The narrator, Charles Hayward, is in love with Aristide's granddaughter and assists the investigating team led by his father, who is Assistant Commissioner at Scotland Yard. The volume measures 190 mm by 120 mm and consists of 192 pages. It is bound in orange cloth, lettered in black. The striking Birtwistle dust-wrapper features a crooked house at night.

A Murder Is Announced

London: Collins, The Crime Club, 1950; New York: Dodd, Mead, 1950

The blue-green dust-wrapper features a clock with the fingers at six-thirty, the time set for the murder in the invitation: 'A murder is announced and will take place on Friday October 29th, at Little Paddocks, at 6.30 pm.' The guests turn up expecting a party game of murder but this one has a real corpse. Fortunately, Jane Marple is staying nearby and, knowing something of the murder victim, involves herself in the case. Christie's fiftieth murder mystery, the book was an instant success. The volume measures 190 mm by 120 mm and consists of 256 pages. It is bound in orange cloth, lettered in black. This year also saw the publication of a set of short stories called *Three Blind Mice* in America. One of these provided an easy adaptation to the stage, becoming the famous production *The Mousetrap*, still performed today.

Above left: Crooked House is the first jacket to show the effect of design changes as the 1950s approached. It could almost be mistaken for a jacket of the 1960s. For once the shy Mrs Christie can be seen on the back cover and on the jacket for *A Murder is Announced*.

Above right: A Murder is Announced is the last jacket to have a pictorial design, as Christie preferred jackets without images that conflicted with her view of the contents.

The 1950s onwards

They Came to Baghdad and **Mrs McGinty's Dead**

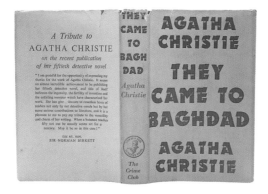 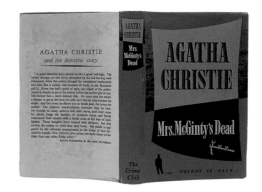

Above left: The jacket for *They Came to Baghdad* is one of most attractive of this period. The typeface is very stylish with the two contrasting complementary colours on the cream background, although it is very prone to becoming dirty.

Above right: As yet unused by film-makers, *Mrs McGinty's Dead* is an excellent story, with real 'bite'. The jacket is quite powerful and looks handsome in red and black.

They Came to Baghdad
London: Collins, The Crime Club, 1951; New York: Dodd, Mead, 1951

Christie's first thriller since *N or M?* is set in Baghdad, which the author knew well from her visits with her archaeologist husband. The heroine, Victoria Jones, sacked from her office job, falls in love with Edward, whose job takes him to Baghdad, the location of a meeting of world leaders which fanatics plan to sabotage. Victoria follows only to have a secret agent die in her hotel room, her yearning for adventure is about to be realized. The volume measures 190 mm by 120 mm and consists of 256 pages. It is bound in orange cloth, lettered in black. The typographical dust-wrapper is lettered in red and green on a buff background.

Mrs McGinty's Dead
London: Collins, The Crime Club, 1952; New York: Dodd, Mead, 1952

An old woman has been bludgeoned to death and her lodger, James Bentley, is found guilty and sentenced to hang. Superintendent Spence persuades Poirot that the verdict is wrong. Poirot discovers the real reason for the murder of the old lady and saves the supremely unattractive Bentley from the long drop. The volume measures 190 mm by 120 mm and consists of 192 pages including four advertisement leaves. It is bound in orange cloth, lettered in black. The mainly typographical dust-wrapper features rust-red lettering shadowed in black on an eau-de-nil ground and white lettering on black inside a axe-head shaped panel split diagonally.

Christie published *A Daughter's Daughter* the same year, under her established Mary Westmacott pen name.

They Do It with Mirrors and After the Funeral

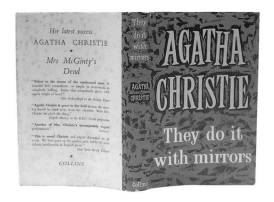 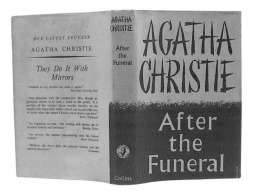

They Do It with Mirrors, London: Collins, The Crime Club, 1952

Murder with Mirrors, New York: Dodd, Mead, 1952

Jane Marple goes to stay with her old friend Carrie Louise at the behest of Ruth, the novel's heroine, who is concerned for her sister's safety. The rambling Victorian mansion also hosts a home for delinquent boys run by Carrie Louise's third husband. An attempt is made to kill the husband; her stepson is murdered and someone tries to poison Carrie Louise herself. Fortunately Miss Marple is on excellent form, and the result is still a firm favourite with her fans. The volume measures 190 mm by 120 mm and consists of 192 pages. It is bound in orange cloth lettered in black. The dust-wrapper features lettering in yellow and white on a purple ground with abstract black patterning.

Above: These first UK edition covers both have an attractive combination of typeface and a simple decorative background. Both are quite hard to find now.

After the Funeral, London: Collins, The Crime Club, 1953

Funerals Are Fatal, New York: Dodd, Mead, 1953

At the reading of the will on the day following the funeral of the wealthy Richard Abernethie, his sister Cora wonders aloud whether his death was suspicious. When Cora is found dead, clearly murdered, the family solicitor decides it might be sensible to recruit the services of Hercule Poirot, who is assisted once more by the eccentric Mr Goby. The volume measures 190 mm by 120 mm and consists of 192 pages. It is bound in orange cloth, lettered in black. The dust-wrapper is typographical with black lettering on the white upper half and white lettering on the lower purple half of the upper panel and spine.

A Pocket Full of Rye and Destination Unknown

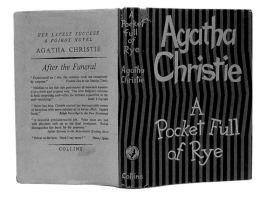 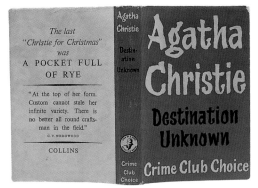

A Pocket Full of Rye

London: Collins, The Crime Club, 1953; New York: Dodd, Mead, 1954

The first person to die is financier Rex Fortescue, at home in Yewtree Lodge, and his wife soon joins him. Following the third death, Jane Marple discerns a murderous pattern in the nursery rhyme 'Sing a song of sixpence, a pocketful of rye…'. She quickly forges a highly effective partnership with the unusually receptive and astute Inspector Neele, who later assists Poirot in *Third Girl*. The volume measures 190 mm by 120 mm and consists of 192 pages (of which page 192 is blank). It is bound in orange cloth, lettered in black. The dust-wrapper features yellow and white lettering on a background of red and black vertical stripes.

Destination Unknown, London: Collins, The Crime Club, 1954

So Many Steps to Death, New York: Dodd, Mead, 1955

Concern grows within the intelligence community when several important scientists disappear. One person may have a lead but dies in a plane crash. Meanwhile, Hilary Craven, planning her suicide in a Casablanca hotel room, is persuaded by a British secret agent that if she must die she may as well do so in the service of her country, and is recruited in the search for the scientists and into some life-affirming adventures. The volume measures 190 mm by 120 mm and consists of 192 pages. It is bound in orange cloth, lettered in black. The rather plain dust-wrapper features black and white lettering on a green background.

Hickory Dickory Dock and Dead Man's Folly

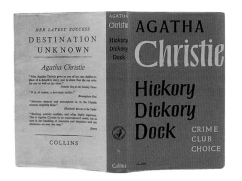 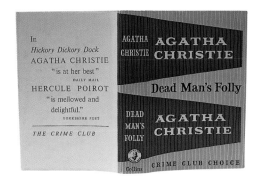

Hickory Dickory Dock, London: Collins, The Crime Club, 1955

Hickory Dickory Death, New York: Dodd, Mead, 1955

The story begins with Poirot's secretary, Felicity Lemon, making mistakes in her typing. Poirot asks her what's wrong and her replies lead him to investigate untoward events at the hostel in Hickory Road managed by Felicity's sister. The problem begins with kleptomania – the list of stolen or damaged objects includes a stethoscope, some old flannel trousers, a slashed rucksack and a diamond ring which turns up in a bowl of soup – but soon becomes a murder investigation. The volume measures 190 mm by 120 mm and consists of 192 pages. It is bound in orange cloth, lettered in black. The dust-wrapper consists of black and white lettering on a salmon-pink background.

Above: The first UK edition of *Hickory Dickory Dock* follows the pattern of *Destination Unknown*, whilst *Dead Man's Folly* is stronger on graphics and typeface.

Dead Man's Folly

London: Collins, The Crime Club, 1956; New York: Dodd, Mead, 1956

The story begins with a village fete in Devon. Christie's alter ego, Ariadne Oliver, agrees to organize a Murder Hunt but is so intimidated by the peculiar local atmosphere that she telephones Poirot, who is sufficiently alarmed to take the first train but cannot prevent the death of the local girl who is to play the part of the body. The volume measures 190 mm by 120 mm and consists of 256 pages. It is bound in orange cloth lettered in black. The dust-wrapper features the author's name in white on two dark-green pennants with black pin-stripes, with the title between in black on a lime-green background with white pin-stripes.

In the same year Christie published her last Mary Westmacott novel, *The Burden*; by now her identity had been revealed.

4.50 FROM PADDINGTON

4.50 from Paddington, London: Collins, The Crime Club, 1957
What Mrs McGillicuddy Saw! New York: Dodd, Mead, 1957

Background

Perhaps unsurprisingly, Christie's American publishers saw fit to change the title, arguing that most American readers were unfamiliar with the names of London's railway stations. Rutherford Hall, where the plot thickens, is yet again based on Christie's beloved Abney Hall in all its Victorian splendour. Abney was the family home of the Watts family and Christie spent many Christmases and holidays there with her best friend and sister in-law, Nan Watts. Abney sits next to the old railway line and the layout of the estate and the interiors are an inspiration for many of the settings in the books. Paddington Station actually serves travel to Devon, on the Great Western line, which runs nowhere near Abney Hall. So Christie simply moves Abney Hall to Devon instead.

Above: Abney Hall, in front of the lake, which also featured in *They Do It with Mirrors* and many of Christie's other novels.

Opposite: Paddington railway station in the early 1950s.

Storyline

Mrs McGillicuddy, travelling down from Scotland on a visit to the village where Jane Marple lives, sees a man throttling a woman on a train passing hers on the adjacent down-main. The action is over very quickly given the speed of the overtaking train but Mrs McGillicuddy is convinced that she had seen a cold-blooded murder. The local police are unimpressed and the only person to accept her story is the redoubtable Jane Marple. It takes some sharp detective work by Miss Marple to persuade the police that murder may have taken place and only with the discovery of a body do they reluctantly become involved.

The main action involves the extended Crackenthorpe family, who own the slightly down-at-heel Rutherford Hall, the grounds of which are bordered at one point by the railway line. Christie plays a little with her devoted readers by having Miss Marple initially declare herself not up to solving another murder, but the detective's pride and her irrepressible curiosity soon combine to change her mind. She is assisted by her great-nephew David, who works for British Railways, and Dermot Craddock, now a detective-inspector at Scotland Yard, whom she first met in *A Murder Is Announced* and with whom she was to work again some years later in *The Mirror Crack'd from Side to Side*. As might be expected, the Crackenthorpes reward investigation and Christie displays her usual skills in lining up suspects, each of whom seems an ideal fit until the next one appears. The murderer is eventually apprehended, though the investigative process seems to rely to some extent on intuition, always a little disappointing for the avid reader. Indeed there are a couple of moments when the age and increasing frailty of Miss Marple are decidedly at odds with the action. She is lucky at one point to avoid being strangled by the murderer and later on manages to interpose herself in unlikely fashion between the murderer and a likely victim.

Book Description

The book is a standard demy-octavo volume measuring 185 mm by 120 mm. It consists of 257 pages, numbered to 256. It is bound in plain red cloth with black lettering on the spine in the usual title – author – imprint order. The Crime Club gunman is not present on the spine of the book but is on the title page facing left as usual. The dust-wrapper is a workmanlike typographical affair using white lettering reversed out of an abstract black and grey background for the author's name and the legend Crime Club Choice, with the

title in white on a red background. The design is carried over onto the spine. The lower panel is given over, as usual, to advertisement. The front inner flap carries the blurb and the price of 12s. 6d.

Reviews

The *New York Herald* did Christie proud: 'Agatha Christie's latest is precisely what one expects: the most delicious bamboozling possible in a babble of bright talk and a comprehensive bristle of suspicion all adeptly managed to keep you too alert elsewhere to see the neat succession of clues that catch a murderer we never so much as thought of.' This neat and sympathetic summary of what might be termed Christie's method was echoed to some extent by the *Times Literary Supplement*, which pointed out, 'Without the female species, indeed, detective fiction would be in a bad way ...' and went on to remind its readers that 'Miss Christie never harrows her readers, being content to intrigue and amuse them.'

Spin-Offs

In 1961, MGM began its series of Miss Marple films with its version of *4.50 from Paddington*, entitled *Murder, She Said*, with a strong cast led by Margaret Rutherford as a rather unlikely Miss Marple. Although the series was well received and Rutherford was popular with the cinema-going public, Christie let it be known that while she regarded Rutherford as a fine actress, she bore no resemblance to her own idea of Miss Marple. To tie in with the release of the film, a new paperback edition of the book was published in the USA with the film title replacing the original. A little over a quarter of century was to pass before the definitive Miss Marple in the form of the actress Joan Hickson starred in the adaptation televised by the BBC and broadcast on Christmas Day 1987, under its original title.

Below: The railway line that lies on the edge of the estate today. The sharp-eyed observer will have noted that one of the tracks has been lifted since the novel was written, for reasons of economy

TORQUAY (Devon)
Miles 199½. Map Sq. 26.
Pop. 53,216. Clos. days Wed. & Sat.
REFRESHMENT ROOMS.
From Paddington.
1st cl.—Single 43/5, Return 86/10.
3rd cl.—Single 28/11, Return 57/10.

Padd.	Torq.	Torq.	Padd.
a.m.		a.m.	
5 30	11 58	12 12b	5 0
7 30r	1 24	12 12d	7 25
9 30r	2 3	7 46r	12 15
12 0r	3 35	8 53r	1 30
p.m.		10 11r	2 50
1 30r	5 51	12 0r	3 35
3 30r	7 42	p.m.	
5 30r	9 47	2 18r	7 10
6 30r	12 6	4 38r	9 0
9 50e	4*25	—	—
11 50e	6 42	—	—
11 50s	6 48	—	—

Sunday Trains.

	a.m.		a.m.
10 30r	2 56	12 12	7 25
p.m.		10 47r	3 45
1 30r	6 0	p.m.	
3 30r	8 30	2 33r	7 20
5 0	9 38	4 39r	9 30
9 50	4*25	8 47	3 25
11 50	6 42	—	—

* Torre Station.
b Monday and Saturday only.
d Not Monday or Saturday.
e Not Saturday.
r Refreshment Car.
s Saturday only.

Above left: The railway bridge on the edge of the estate over which runs the railway line, from which the murderer threw the body onto the embankment.

Above centre: The clock at Paddington station at the appointed hour of departure.

Above right: Train times to Torquay from Paddington in *The ABC Railway Guide.* Abney Hall could not actually be reached from Paddington station but Christie transplanted her fictionalized house to Devon.

Below: The first-edition dust-jacket, relying entirely on typefaces for effect. This is one of the more pleasing results.

A case for
HERCULE POIROT
in
DEAD MAN'S
FOLLY

"A classic Christie and one
of the best."
Elizabeth Bowen

THE CRIME CLUB

AGATHA
CHRISTIE
4·50
From
Paddington

AGATHA
CHRISTIE
4·50 FROM
PADDINGTON

Collins CRIME CLUB CHOICE

4.50 from Paddington • 211

Ordeal by Innocence and
Cat Among the Pigeons

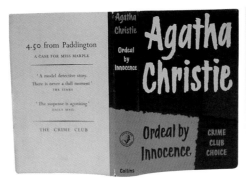 

Ordeal by Innocence

London: Collins, The Crime Club, 1958; New York: Dodd, Mead, 1959

One of Christie's own favourites, this story concerns belated justice. Arthur Calgary returns from an expedition to the Antarctic to discover that the man who was found guilty of the murder of his mother has died in prison. Had he been available, he could have provided an alibi and prevented a miscarriage of justice. His admission provokes a second death before the truth is discovered. The volume measures 190 mm by 120 mm and consists of 256 pages. It is bound in orange cloth, lettered in black. The dust-wrapper features white lettering on black over three-quarters of the upper panel, the remaining quarter displaying black lettering on an orange ground.

Cat Among the Pigeons

London: Collins, The Crime Club, 1959; New York: Dodd, Mead, 1960

This is one of Christie's best later novels, combining two disparate plots. In a Middle Eastern state in turmoil, a prince gives his pilot jewels to smuggle into England. Before this can happen both men die. Meanwhile, a frightened schoolgirl recruits Poirot to discover who is killing off the staff at her school. Poirot takes revolution in Ramat and the summer term at Meadowbank entirely in his stride. The volume measures 190 mm by 120 mm and consists of 256 pages. It is bound in orange cloth, lettered in black. The upper panel of the dust-wrapper features white lettering against a pattern of blue and purple rectangles outlined in black.

The Adventure of the Christmas Pudding
and The Pale Horse

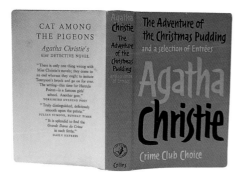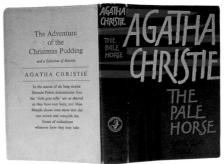

The Adventure of the Christmas Pudding
London: Collins, The Crime Club, 1960

The book contains six stories, the first five featuring Poirot and the last Jane Marple. The author wishes her readers a Happy Christmas and then proceeds with relish to deliver generous helpings of murder and mayhem. The title story has Poirot reluctantly spending Christmas at an English country-house and managing, despite being force-fed, to rise to the discovery of a body in the snow. Jane Marple offers a suitably light and frothy finale. The volume measures 190 mm by 120 mm and consists of 256 pages. It is bound in orange cloth, lettered in black. The upper panel of the dust-wrapper features black, white and yellow lettering on a light-brown background.

Above: The Pale Horse jacket uses a design formula employed several times with success. *The Adventure of the Christmas Pudding* is an enjoyable set of short stories, though the wrapper is a totally different layout from usual.

The Pale Horse
London: Collins, The Crime Club, 1961; New York: Dodd, Mead, 1962

The title, a biblical synonym for Death, is the name of an organization which kills by black magic and the name of a house, formerly an inn, in the local village. A priest summoned to attend a dying woman is later murdered. A list of names is found and the narrator, Mark Easterbrook, discovers unsuspected connections. Ariadne Oliver, a friend, assists but, for once, the police solve the mystery. The volume measures 190 mm by 12 mm and consists of 256 pages. It is bound in orange cloth, lettered in black. The charcoal-grey dust-wrapper features white lettering over lateral red spears and light-blue lettering alongside vertical black spears.

The Mirror Crack'd from Side to Side and **The Clocks**

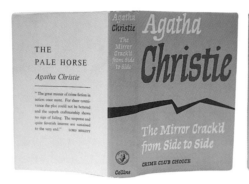 

The Mirror Crack'd from Side to Side, London: Collins, The Crime Club, 1962

The Mirror Crack'd, New York: Dodd, Mead, 1963

Above left: The first UK jacket of *The Mirror Crack'd from Side to Side,* a famous Miss Marple mystery, though again the jacket tells one little about the content.

Above right: The Clocks shows an effective use of 1960s graphics and has a stronger impact.

All is not well in St Mary Mead. Gossington Hall has been sold to a Hollywood starlet, with the widowed Dolly Bantry banished to the East Lodge. At a fete in the grounds, a guest dies after swallowing a poisoned drink, and other murders follow. Fortunately, Jane Marple is still there to assist the police with the unravelling of the plot. The volume measures 190 mm by 120 mm and consists of 256 pages. It is bound in orange cloth lettered in black. The upper panel of the dust-wrapper consists of white, red and black lettering on a pea-green background with the upper half separated from the lower by a jagged black line.

The Clocks

London: Collins, The Crime Club, 1963; New York: Dodd, Mead, 1964

The story begins with the murder of a man in a clock-filled room in the seaside resort of Crowdean. Strangely, the woman who finds the body hears a cuckoo clock strike three – but the four clocks in the room all say 4.13. Colin Lamb, a passer-by, involves Poirot, an old friend of his father, Superintendent Battle. Poirot triumphs, but not before delivering a fascinating disquisition on the art of detection, true and fictional. The volume measures 190 mm by 120 mm and consists of 256 pages. It is bound in orange cloth, lettered in black. The upper panel of the John Harvey dust-wrapper consists of black and orange lettering on a white ground; the lower part features the black hands of a clock against a blue background.

A Caribbean Mystery
and At Bertram's Hotel

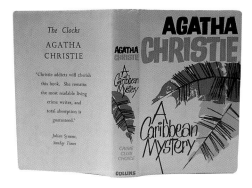 

A Caribbean Mystery
London: Collins, The Crime Club, 1964; New York: Dodd, Mead, 1965

Jane Marple, who has been unwell, is sent by her solicitous nephew on holiday to the West Indies. Despite the exotic setting, little time elapses before her formidable powers are put to the test with the death, in suspicious circumstances, of Major Palgrave, an elderly fellow guest. Miss Marple rises to the occasion splendidly, impressing in the process another elderly guest, Mr Rafiel, whom she will encounter again in *Nemesis*. The volume measures 190 mm by 120 mm and consists of 256 pages. It is bound in red cloth, lettered in gilt. The upper panel of the dust-wrapper features orange and black lettering on a white ground with yellow and blue palm-tree branches. Christie also published *Star Over Bethlehem*, a set of short stories and poems, in this year.

At Bertram's Hotel
London: Collins, The Crime Club, 1965; New York: Dodd, Mead, 1966

Once more the kindly nephew underwrites a holiday for Aunt Jane. Offered a fortnight at Bournemouth, Miss Marple opts for a week at Bertram's, a delightfully old-fashioned hotel modelled on Brown's in the heart of Mayfair. The pace is leisurely and time is taken to develop a diverse range of characters, both staff and guests. There is inevitably a murder and it is left to Miss Marple to point the way to the amiable Chief Inspector Davy. The volume measures 190 mm by 120 mm and contains 256 pages. It is bound in red cloth and lettered gilt. The upper panel of the dust-wrapper features black and white lettering on asymmetric blue and green panels on a white ground.

Above: A Caribbean Mystery has an attractive jacket, displaying a fresh approach and giving a pleasant flavour of the plot, though being cream it is prone to becoming dirty and rubbed.

At Bertram's Hotel relies completely on typeface and colour for effect.

Third Girl and Endless Night

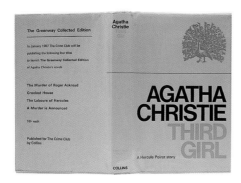 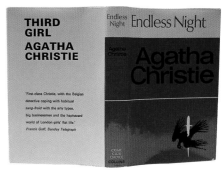

Above: Both first UK editions now rely on the simplest form of colour, shading and typeface. This style was typical of the 1970s, but unfortunately doesn't communicate the contents as well as the earlier designs, therefore perhaps losing some of their charm.

Third Girl

London: Collins, The Crime Club, 1966; New York: Dodd, Mead, 1967

Poirot, having finished his magnum opus on the great writers of detective fiction, welcomes the arrival of a young woman at his flat 'about a murder she might have committed'. Unfortunately, Norma Restarick takes one look at Poirot and leaves, on the grounds that he is too ancient to be of any use. Later that day, over tea with his friend Ariadne Oliver, Poirot learns that it was Ariadne who had sent Norma to his flat and the two decide to work together to establish whether Norma, who has now vanished into thin air, apparently missed by nobody, is guilty or innocent of the 'murder', or merely deluded. The critics liked the book. The *Times Literary Supplement* wrote, 'Hercule Poirot is sadly worried about getting old ... but it is still a pleasure to watch cher maitre at work.' The *New York Times* wrote, 'Poirot returns ... that should be enough to send you scurrying to the bookstore. The plot is only moderately good Christie ... But Poirot is as absurd and as able as ever.'

Endless Night

London: Collins, The Crime Club, 1967; New York: Dodd, Mead, 1968

In this novel, liked by Christie and critics alike, Michael Rogers, a drifter from humble beginnings, dreams of a rich beautiful wife and of building the perfect house for her. One day he discovers a decrepit house in a beautiful setting called Gipsy's Acre, which is for sale. While walking the site, he meets a beautiful (and rich) young woman who has also fallen in love with Gipsy's Acre. They fall to discussing its potential. Before long they are married and an architect is commissioned to build the house of their dreams there. But the curse of Gipsy's Acre strikes and death intervenes.

By the Pricking of My Thumbs and Hallowe'en Party

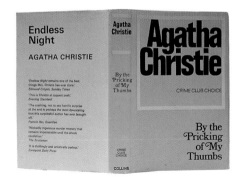 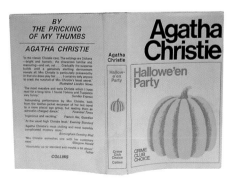

By the Pricking of My Thumbs

London: Collins, The Crime Club, 1968; New York: Dodd, Mead, 1968

While the Beresfords are visiting an aged aunt in a nursing home, Tuppence chats to some of the inmates, including Mrs Lancaster, who notices Tuppence looking at the fireplace and remarks, 'I see you're looking at the fireplace – was it your poor child?' After Aunt Ada's death, they come across a painting of a house given to her by Mrs Lancaster. The pair set out to discover the truth behind Mrs Lancaster's words and find the real house, which is more sinister than the painted version, and an old woman who is less senile than she seems.

Hallowe'en Party

London: Collins, The Crime Club, 1969; New York: Dodd, Mead, 1969.

Ariadne Oliver is staying with a friend at their home in the stockbroker belt. It is Hallowe'en time and they go off to help at a party for young people nearby. Ariadne, who has a passion for apples, helps set up the apple bob in the library. When the guests learn that they have a famous crime writer among them, they ply Ariadne with questions. One difficult adolescent called Joyce complains that Ariadne's last book didn't have enough blood in it and remarks that she observed a murder once. Nobody believes her and Joyce storms off. While the party is in full swing in the drawing-room, Joyce is drowned in the apple-bobbing tub. The murder is condemned as the act of a maniac but Ariadne is not convinced. She seeks the help of Poirot, who is very sympathetic: 'The victim is always important … the victim, you see, is so often the cause of the crime.' The reviews were mixed. The *Times Literary Supplement* commented, 'Clever old Agatha Christie is still plodding along her well-trodden but engaging track … Unusually with Mrs Christie, you can guess who did it.'

Above: Both jackets have the plain pastel shades fashionable at the time and largely consist of type that is easy to read from some distance, with a simple background.

By the Pricking of My Thumbs; Hallowe'en Party • 217

Passenger to Frankfurt and Nemesis

 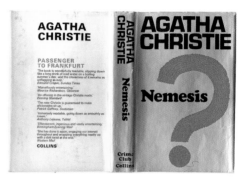

Passenger to Frankfurt

London: Collins, The Crime Club, 1970; New York: Dodd, Mead, 1970

The publication celebrated Christie's eightieth birthday and, although couched in the language of a thriller, says much about the author's world-view. A senior diplomat, Sir Stafford Nye, is waiting for a flight at Frankfurt when he is approached by a young woman with an extraordinary proposal. She wants him to take a drugged drink which will allow her to borrow his cloak and passport so she can escape to England. Nye, bored and world weary, agrees. When he wakes up, he reports the theft and returns to England, where two attempts are made on his life. He re-establishes contact with the young woman and soon finds himself back in Germany with her in pursuit of a group bent on world domination. Crime fiction expert A. J. Hubin, writing in the *New York Times,* spoke for many when he commented, 'The book doesn't really come off; in fact it doesn't come off at all. This is doubly sad because I suspect Miss Christie has thrown more of herself into this book than any other.'

Nemesis

London: Collins, The Crime Club, 1971; New York: Dodd, Mead, 1971

Miss Marple notes the name of Jason Rafiel in the obituary column of *The Times.* Soon afterwards, his solicitors write to her offering a legacy of £20,000, provided she investigates a crime. The letter is short on detail but is followed by an invitation to join a tour of English houses and gardens at the expense of the late Mr Rafiel. Miss Marple joins the tour and it is not long before she is on the scent of a crime from Jason Rafiel's past. The critics were kind. The *Times Literary Supplement* enjoyed meeting Miss Marple again, 'an old lady now, of course … but still capable, at a dead man's behest, of taking …. a mystery coach tour [as her] dead benefactor hoped she would'.

218 • The 1950s onwards

Elephants Can Remember and Postern of Fate

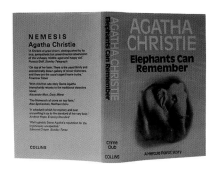 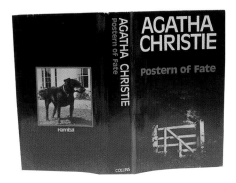

Elephants Can Remember
London: Collins, The Crime Club, 1972; New York: Dodd, Mead, 1972

Ariadne Oliver is cornered at a literary luncheon, by the supremely bossy Mrs Burton-Cox, who is determined to interrogate her about Ariadne's goddaughter Celia, a young woman whose parents had died in tragic circumstances and who is engaged to be married to her son Desmond. Her prospective mother-in-law insists on discovering the truth: had Celia Ravencroft's father murdered her mother and then committed suicide or vice versa? Ariadne seeks help from Hercule Poirot for the final time (if we discount the 'last' Poirot written many years previously but published later). Together they delve into the past. Reviews were barely polite. In the *New York Times Book Review*, Newgate Callendar concluded, 'This is vintage Christie. But it is, alas, not very good.'

Above: In a gesture to earlier jackets, here a refreshing attempt is made to depict the plots. Compared to other contemporary jacket designs, such as those for the novels of Colin Dexter, first published in 1974, these are still very simple.

Postern of Fate
London: Collins, The Crime Club, 1973; New York: Dodd, Mead, 1973

This was to be Christie's last novel, although several books written earlier remained unpublished. Tommy and Tuppence move to a new home, the Laurels, where Tuppence finds a collection of children's books left by a former owner. One of them has letters underlined which decoded read, 'Mary Jordan did not die naturally'. Enquiries reveal that Mary Jordan, who lived at the Laurels, was suspected of being mixed up with secrets involving a new submarine. Someone does not want her death investigated but they have reckoned without the arthritic duo, who solve their final mystery with help from some familiar characters. The reviews were crushing. In the *New York Times Book Review* Newgate Callendar felt obliged to comment, 'It is sad to see a veteran author working under nothing but momentum. [The book] is a contrived affair that creeps from dullness to boredom.'

Poirot's Early Cases and Curtain

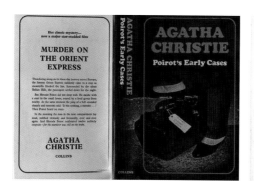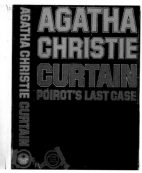

Above left: Poirot's Early Cases is one of the best 1970s designs. The black background with the Cooper Black typeface adds strength and it is becoming quite hard to find these days.

Above right: Curtain, which sees Poirot's final appearance, is one of the boldest designs, emphasizing the impact of the plot by its likeness to a spy thriller.

Hercule Poirot's Early Cases
London: Collins, The Crime Club, 1974; New York: Dodd, Mead, 1974

In place of the usual novel, given her advancing years, Christie's publishers brought out a collection of eighteen short stories written in the inter-war years and earlier serialized in newspapers or magazines. Roughly contemporaneous with *Poirot Investigates*, they are in no respect inferior to that collection, published fifty years previously. Fourteen of the stories are narrated by Hastings, the remainder were written after his creator banished him to Argentina. *Publishers Weekly* enjoyed the collection: 'fine wine in a new bottle for aficionados of the mistress of mystery. It's exhilarating to be back in the company of the Belgian dandy, Poirot, as the little grey cells land him again and again one meaningful step ahead of crook, cop and reader. As always, the author is scrupulously fair with her audience – the clues are all there – but she invariably surprises us just the same.'

Curtain: Poirot's Last Case
London: Collins, The Crime Club, 1975; New York: Dodd, Mead, 1975

With nothing new to offer, Collins approached Christie for permission to publish one of the two books she had written during the Blitz and kept aside as a legacy for her daughter Rosalind. After some resistance, William Collins persuaded Christie that she should have the last word with Poirot. Appropriately Hastings, Poirot's oldest friend, narrates and the action takes place at Styles, although it has fallen on hard times and is now a hotel. Poirot, now confined to a wheelchair, exercises the little grey cells for the last time, against a formidable murderer. The reviews were, with the occasional peevish exception, generous. Francis Wyndham in the *Times Literary Supplement* wrote for many: 'The solution, when it is finally sprung, turns out to be as outrageously satisfying as [her best]. As she presumably intended, in this one [she] has brought off the bluff to end them all.'

Sleeping Murder and Miss Marple's Final Cases

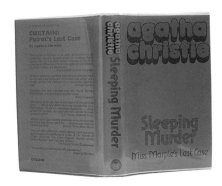

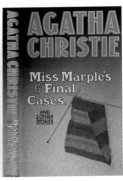

Sleeping Murder

London: Collins, The Crime Club, 1976; New York: Dodd, Mead, 1976

This was the second of the two wartime books which had been salted away. Gwenda Reed moves into Hillside, a charming Victorian villa, but strange happenings make her suspect the house is haunted. The climax happens during a performance of *The Duchess of Malfi*. At the words 'Cover her face; mine eyes dazzle: she died young', she has a vision of a man declaiming the same lines as he stands over the body of a woman lying at the foot of the Hillside stairs. Later she unburdens herself to Jane Marple, a guest at the performance, and together they solve an old crime. The reviews were mixed. In the *Times Literary Supplement* T. J. Binyon wrote, '*Sleeping Murder* has all the virtues of Agatha Christie's work: a coherent plot, firm and purposeful narration, and a pleasant, light and agreeable style. On the other hand, the red herrings are not as convincing as they might be.'

Miss Marple's Final Cases

London: Collins, The Crime Club, 1979

The book contains six Miss Marple short stories and two others, all of which had appeared in the USA in collections of detective stories and in the UK in serial form. This was their first appearance in the UK as a collection in book form. The stories are all very readable but come from mid-career and strictly speaking are not Miss Marple's last cases. The reviewer in *The Times* wrote, 'The stories are not all perfect. A decided aroma of the confectioner's comes from some. But the best two or three, simply recounted, not in any way overloaded with significances that would be better in a novel, yet not underloaded either by having characters too sketchy or too cobbled together to satisfy, are simply what this sort of thing should be. When you finish one you feel you have come to the end not that you have got to the end.'

Above left: The first edition of *Sleeping Murder* has a plain purple-pink cover with bubble writing and is quite unrelated to the story, which was completed during the war and so had all the quality of Christie's early novels.

Above right: The jacket for *Miss Marple's Final Cases* consists just of a photograph of the famous sleuth's trademark, her much-loved knitting.

BIBLIOGRAPHY

Burton, Anthony, *The Orient Express: The History of the Orient Express Service from 1883 to 1950,* David & Charles, 2001

Cade, Jared, *The Eleven Missing Days,* Peter Owen Publishing, 1995

Christie, Agatha, *An Autobiography,* Collins, 1977

Cooper, John, and Pike, B. A., *Detective Fiction: The Collector's Guide,* second edition, Scolar Press, 1994

Cooper, John, and Pike, B. A., *Artists in Crime: An Illustrated Survey of Crime Fiction First Edition Dust-wrappers, 1920–1970,* Scolar Press, 1995

Dowsett, Alan, *History of the Handley Page 42,* Tempus Publishing, 2003

Jaspert, W. P., Berry, W. T. and Johnson, A. F., *Encyclopaedia of Type Faces,* Blandford Press, 1953, Cassell Paperbacks, 1990

Knight, Stephen, *Form and Ideology in Crime Fiction,* Macmillan, 1980

McCall, Henrietta, *Agatha Christie and Archaeology* (exhibition catalogue), British Museum Press, 2001

McCall, Henrietta, *Max Mallowan,* British Museum Press, 2001

Mallowan, Max, *Autobiography,* Collins, 1977

Morgan, Janet, *Agatha Christie,* Collins, 1984

Osborne, Charles, *The Life and Crimes of Agatha Christie,* Collins, 1982

Watson, Colin, *Snobbery with Violence: English Crime Stories and Their Audience,* revised and reprinted, Eyre Methuen, 1979

Articles from the Royal Pharmaceutical Society Journals and Magazines, London, 1920–1985

Research material provided by Croydon Airport Archives, Surrey

Research material on Abney Hall provided by Stockport Heritage Library, Cheshire

The author and publishers have made every effort to trace and contact the owners of copyright material used in this book; in a few instances this has not been possible and anyone claiming ownership of material reproduced here should contact the publishers.

CREDITS

Idea, photography, jacket design, content design & construction, research & captions: Vanessa Wagstaff.
Body text and text research: Stephen Poole.
Typefaces used: *Adobe Garamond family, Anarcharsis, Basuto, DH Sans, Gill Sans family.*
All photographs & design © Vanessa Wagstaff Picture Library except for the following as listed: b=bottom; t=top; l=left; r=right; c= centre

All UK dust jackets and title pages reproduced throughout, from 1926 to 1978, and pages 90l, 136, extract p.146 Mallowan, Max, Autobiography, 1977, with very kind permission © HarperCollins, London; Extracts and quotations from Agatha Christie works reproduced with kind permission of Agatha Christie Ltd, a Chorion Company. All rights reserved. Venice Simplon Orient Express © Wagon Lits Diffusion, Paris, 2003: 89, 90; reproduced by kind permission of the copyright owners, © OAG Worldwide Ltd: 74, 111, 113, 120, 211; Croydon Airport Photographic Archives ©: 58, 59, 102t and br, 104, 105, 107tr, 108tr, 121 tr, 149, all with endorsement from British Airways Archives; © Carlotta Barrow, and with permission of Carnival Films, London: 16b, 25b, 29, 32, 33, 36, 112b, 144t and cl, 173; © Charlotte Holdich: 44c; © copyright of The Trustees of the British Museum: 120, 121b, 124; © copyright John Mallowan, 119 t&b, 130b, 133t and bl, 138 appear with very kind permission; 147 © Jane Taylor [Petra]; 140 © JDHT [Jaguar Archives]; Stockport Heritage Library © 156t, 188, 192t, 209tr and b; John Lane, The Bodley Head dust jackets and title pages from 1920–1925, © kind permission of Random House Group Ltd; 26, fade © Clarissa Dann; 9, 10tl, 16t, 17t, 20b, 85br, 108tl, 151cl, 176 bl, © with kind permission from The Museum of the Royal Pharmaceutical Society; 206 © The Science and Society Picture Library, London. © Rex Morgan with very kind permission: 10, Agatha Christie by Charles Morgan.

Websites of note: www.artdesign-vjwagstaff.com; www.biblion.com; www.burghisland.com; www.facsimiledustjackets.com; www.jamesmpickard.com; www.hoptoncourt.co.uk

INDEX